C000301739

PRES'

NORTH END F.C.

– THE 25 YEAR RECORD

1971-72 to 1995-96 Seasons

SEASON BY SEASON WRITE-UPS
David Powter

EDITOR
Michael Robinson

British Library Cataloguing in Publication Data
A catalogue record for this book is available from the British Library

ISBN 0-947808-80-9

Copyright © 1996; SOCCER BOOK PUBLISHING LTD. (01472-696226)
72, St. Peters' Avenue, Cleethorpes, N.E. Lincolnshire, DN35 8HU, England

All rights are reserved. No part of this publication may be reproduced, stored into a retrieval system
or transmitted, in any form or by any means, electronic, mechanical, photocopying, recording, or
otherwise, without the prior written permission of Soccer Book Publishing Ltd.

Printed by Redwood Books, Kennet House, Kennet Way, Trowbridge, Wilts.

CONTENTS

PRESTON NORTH END
– Seasons 1971-72 to 1995-96

Preston North End completed the most traumatic 25 seasons in their history by deservedly securing the 1995-96 Third Division title, under the stewardship of Gary Peters. It was this great club's first trophy since they won the old Third Division in 1971, when managed by Alan Ball Senior. In the intervening period the Football League's first Champions experienced four relegations and were promoted on three occasions.

The Lilywhites' return to the Second Division in 1971-72 was quite a bumpy one and they only avoided relegation by three points, in 18th place, on the back of their respectable early season home form. They only won one League game on their travels (at Ayresome Park) and stumbled badly during their last nine fixtures, losing seven and winning just once – the return match with Middlesbrough. The joint top scorers were Alan Tarbuck and the much-travelled Hugh McIlmoyle (with ten apiece). Over 27,000 thronged Deepdale for the local derby with Burnley, but the ground's biggest gate of the season was for the F.A. Cup fourth round clash with Manchester United. A crowd of 37,052 watched United win 2-0 with a brace by Alan Gowling, who in 1982-83 would don a North End shirt.

Goals were in short supply (only 37 in total) during the following campaign with Preston scoring more than once on only nine occasions. Ball lost his job in February 1973 following four heavy defeats. Despite winning only one of their last 17 fixtures, relegation was again avoided, in 1972-73, as they finished 19th, just one point above the less fortunate Huddersfield Town.

Preston's new manager was Bobby Charlton, following his emotional departure from Old Trafford. The former England maestro recruited three of his old United colleagues – Francis Burns, Nobby Stiles and David Sadler, all internationals – to bolster his squad. One man to depart Deepdale during the course of the season was Alex Bruce. The Scot had been the club's top scorer the previous term (with 13) and, despite transferring to Newcastle United in the January, he also headed the 1973-74 scorers' list with 9.

Bruce's departure sounded the relegation knell for the Lilywhites who failed to score in nine of the remaining 16 fixtures. They slipped back to the Third

Division in 21st place – having won only nine times in an unhappy season. Goalkeeper Alan Kelly made his 447th and last League appearance (a club record) for North End in 1973-74, but stayed at Deepdale in a coaching capacity.

Charlton donned his boots again the following campaign and appeared in each of the first 38 games. His side made a very promising start and looked on course to return to the second-flight at the first attempt. They still led the table at the end of October before fading into the pack on the back of four successive defeats. They stayed in promotion contention until the spring, but won only two of their last 14 games to finish 1974-75 in ninth place – six points short of their promotion target. Mel Holden top scored with 17 goals, while Tony Morley and Mike Elwiss netted ten apiece. The number '2' shirt was worn in the last three games by local lad Mark Lawrenson.

Deepdale was rocked by Charlton's departure in August 1975 after a dispute with the board regarding the transfer of centre-back John Bird to Newcastle, the deal having been struck without the manager's knowledge. Former Everton boss Harry Catterick took over the reins and the early season results suggested a promotion push was on the cards. However, Preston's form had again ebbed away by the November Bermuda Triangle, and a spell of one win in nine outings pushed them into the bottom half of the table by mid-January.

Catterick's side worked their back up to finish eighth, eight points short of a promotion place. Elwiss netted 15 goals to be joint top-scorer with Bruce who had returned to Deepdale in the early part of 1975-76 after a fairly fruitless spell St James' Park.

Preston made a rather ignominious exit from the F.A. Cup at the second round stage at the hands of Scarborough. The then Northern Premier outfit won 3-2 on the East Coast to inflict Preston's first defeat by a Non-League side for 63 years.

Bruce thumped 24 goals (and Elwiss 19) as Preston went even closer to regaining their second-flight place in 1976-77. However, they finished five points short and had to be content with sixth place. A poor start impeded them, but promotion was still very much a possibility until they lost four successive games at the start of April.

The promising Lawrenson moved to Brighton during the close season, while Catterick retired and was succeeded by chief coach Nobby Stiles. The former

England wing-half steered Preston to promotion at his first attempt when they finished third with 56 points, the same number as Peterborough United (who were shaded out on goal difference). Bruce (27) and Elwiss (11) again contributed the bulk of the goals, while ever-present goalkeeper Roy Tunks was beaten only 38 times. The veteran Alan Spavin reappeared on five occasions, but generally North End fielded a settled side with ten men appearing 30 or more times. The other key members of the 1977-78 squad were Burns, Stephen Doyle, Gordon Coleman, Sean Haselgrave, John McMahon, Graham Cross and Michael Baxter.

After wining one and drawing three of the first five Division Two fixtures, North End hit a disastrous patch in 1978-79 when they collected just two points in ten games. With Bruce (21) and Michael Robinson (13) netting on a regular basis, Stiles' side lost only four more times, in the final two thirds of the campaign, to finish in a respectable seventh place. Spavin made his 424th and last appearance during the 1978-79 campaign.

Deepdale tasted a little F.A. Cup glory in 1978-79 when First Division Derby were defeated 3-0 in the third round, a brace by Bruce and another by Burns inflicting the damage. However, another top-flight side, Southampton, ended the Lilywhites' interest in the competition in the next tie.

Robinson moved to Manchester City during the summer of 1979, with Preston receiving a club record fee of £765,000. North End spent the majority of the following campaign in the top half of the table; but a lack of consistency prevented them making a serious push for promotion. A mammoth 19 matches were drawn and they finished 1979-80 in 10th place. Steve Elliott headed the scorers' list with 16.

Stiles' four year reign at Deepdale came to an end in the summer of 1981 after the club slipped back to the Third Division in 20th place on goal difference. The Lilywhites won only 11 games all term, including three of the last six – one of which was the final rearranged fixture at Derby. However, Cardiff City's goalless draw on the same day proved just enough to send North End down. An inability to find the net was the major problem in 1980-81, Bruce top scoring with 13 out of an inadequate tally of 41.

The new manager was Tommy Docherty – one of the club's best players in the 1950s. The Doc's stay was to be a brief one – he was sacked in early December after leading Preston to just three victories in 17 League games. Gordon Lee was soon appointed as Docherty's successor and results improved in the new year. They finished 1981-82 in 14th place, with 18 goal Bruce yet again top scoring.

Preston's start to 1982-83 mirrored that of twelve months earlier, with only three victories coming from 17 games. However, Lee weathered the storm and relegation was avoided, in 16th place, on the back of a run of nine wins from their final 13 fixtures. Elliott top scored with 19; Bruce netted seven times to take his Preston total to 157 goals (from 363 League games) before moving to Wigan Athletic.

Only one of the first 15 fixtures was won in 1983-84, with seven successive defeats pushing North End into the relegation zone. So it was hardly a surprise when Gordon Lee was sacked in December 1983. Club coach and former Republic of Ireland boss Alan Kelly was appointed the new manager. Although Kelly made no new signings, his side showed better form and finished in 16th place. Elliott was again the top-scorer (with 16).

The 1984-85 campaign started on an optimistic note with four victories in the first five games. However, this only paved the way for a barren spell of seven successive defeats which sent Preston plummeting into the relegation zone. Kelly's side never recovered and they also crashed to an ignominious second round F.A. Cup defeat at the hands of non-League Telford United. The Alliance side travelled north to Deepdale and secured a resounding 4-1 win.

After spending 27 years at the club in various capacities, Kelly bade farewell in April 1985. The new man at the helm was the player-coach Tommy Booth. The former Manchester City centre-half was unable to carry out the mission impossible – to save the Football League's initial Champions from tumbling into the Fourth Division for the first time. However, it was a close thing, for although they finished in 23rd place, they only finished one point behind 'safe' Swansea City.

Booth failed to get Preston back on an even keel and was sacked the following January with the club lying one off the bottom of the League. His former assistant Brian Kidd was appointed manager; but the new regime lasted just two days short of two months. Kidd resigned with the club propping up the whole League. Midfielder Jonathan Clark took over on a temporary basis and a burst of five successive victories enabled the Lilywhites to move off the bottom. They finished 1985-86 in 23rd place, with John Thomas hitting 17 goals to be top scorer. For the only time in their history, the Lilywhites had to apply for re-election, but were voted back into the fold.

Thomas was also the main marksman (with 21) twelve months later, as Preston strode to promotion under new manager John McGrath. They were always in the slipstream of long-term leaders Northampton Town, but lost only eight times and finished as runners-up with a club record 90 points. Gary Brazil was the second top scorer (with 17), while the other key members of McGrath's 1986-87 squad were Alex Jones (who was ever present), Sam Allardyce, Les Chapman, Bob Atkins, Michael Bennett, Oshor Williams, Gary Swann and Ron Hildersley. Goalkeeping duties were shared by David Brown and Alan Kelly (the 18 year old son of). The 1986-87 campaign was the first after Preston installed a plastic pitch.

With Thomas joining Bolton Wanderers, Preston's fire-power was diminished and they struggled in the Third Division in 1987-88. They won just four of their first 22 fixtures, but improved to climb out of relegation trouble and finish 16th. Brazil top scored with 14 out of 48.

North End made a mediocre start to 1988-89, but six victories in eight games propelled them up to third in early November. They only won four of their next 15 fixtures, but regained their form to finish in a play-off berth in sixth place. However, their promotion chance evaporated when Port Vale defeated them 3-1 in the semi-final second leg (after the Deepdale leg had finished all-square).

McGrath departed midway through 1989-90 following poor League form and a 2-0 F.A. Cup second round exit at Northern Premier League Whitley Bay. His assistant Les Chapman stepped forward to steer Preston clear of the drop. They had struggled after failing to recover from a poor start, but just scrambled to safety in 19th place, two points clear of relegation.

The following campaign was also rather undistinguished although Chapman's side finished two places higher in 17th. Graham Shaw finished 1990-91 as the top scorer on the 10 goal mark, after netting six times in the final 11 fixtures.

Shaw was again the main marksman (with 14) when North End also finished 17th twelve months later. Five successive draws hampered their early season progress and a pointless January ensured that they finished 1991-92 nearer the wrong end of the table than the top.

The board's patience with Chapman finally expired at the end of September

1992. Eleven weeks later John Beck was appointed in his place and the ex-Cambridge United boss quickly made wholesale changes.

Beck's new look side initially had mixed fortunes, but relegation looked to have been avoided until a disastrous pointless final five fixtures, which included 4-1 and 5-1 home defeats by Leyton Orient and Mansfield Town, respectively. Preston finished three points short of safety and crashed back into the basement, in 21st place, despite being the Second Division's ninth highest scorers (with 65 goals - 22 of which were netted by Tony Ellis) in 1992-93.

Ellis was the Division's top scorer (with 26) in the next campaign. Preston headed the Third Division table at the end of November 1993, after winning 11 of their first 16 fixtures. Yet, they suffered a major loss of momentum, winning just once in their next 11 outings and eventually slipped down to fifth, six points short of an automatic promotion place. However, promotion in 1993-94 was still a possibility via the play-off route. Despite losing 2-0 at Torquay in the semi-final first leg, North End reached Wembley with a rousing 4-1 victory in the return match at Deepdale.

The final was a super game; but the Football League's original Champions were defeated 4-2 by its newest recruits – Wycombe Wanderers. Beck's side belied their long-ball reputation to play some attractive football and scored two classy first half goals. Ian Bryson's outrageous bicycle-kick was immediately equalised, but a majestic header by Paul Raynor restored the Lancastrian lead. Nevertheless, Wycombe's scintillating second half display consigned the Lilywhites to a longer spell in the basement.

After eight seasons of being plastic, the Deepdale pitch was restored to grass during the summer of 1994. The disappointment of missing out at Wembley, followed by seven successive defeats, took the wind out of Preston's sails in the early part of the following campaign. The long ball approach attracted increased criticism and Beck resigned, in early December, rather than change his tactics. His assistant Gary Peters steeped up to take the reins and began with four successive victories. The Lilywhites gradually moved into play-off contention and met that target by again finishing fifth. However, there was to be no repeat Wembley appearance, in 1994-95, as North End disappointed in the play-off semi-final, Bury winning both legs 1-0.

Preston gave no thought to the play-offs in 1995-96 as, playing attractive football, they clinched automatic promotion and were then crowned

Champions. Peters' side shrugged off a sluggish start to move into the top three in October. They then showed tremendous consistency to edge past leaders Gillingham in the March, and held on to take the title by three points.

The key members of the 1995-96 Third Division Championship winning squad were goalkeeper John Vaughan, Bryson, Simon Davey, David Moyes, Steve Wilkinson, Russell Wilcox, Graeme Atkinson and 29 goal Andy Saville (the Division's joint top scorer).

With the antique West Stand replaced by the superb new 8,000 seater Tom Finney Stand in early 1996, Preston North End marched forward with great optimism, and have a fresh look both on and off the field.

Above – Deepdale pictured during the days of the 'plastic pitch'.
Below – the new Tom Finney Stand opened in 1996.

1971-72

1	Aug	14	(a)	Carlisle U	D	0-0		11,063
2		21	(h)	Fulham	W	2-0	McIlmoyle 2	16,425
3		28	(a)	Luton T	D	1-1	Heppolette	11,772
4		30	(h)	Burnley	L	1-3	McIlmoyle (pen)	27,284
5	Sep	4	(h)	Oxford U	W	1-0	McIlmoyle	12,891
6		11	(a)	Q.P.R.	L	1-2	Ham	13,578
7		18	(h)	Charlton Ath	W	2-1	Clarke, Ham	13,198
8		25	(a)	Sunderland	L	3-4	Ham, McIlmoyle (pen), Lyall	13,102
9		28	(h)	Norwich C	L	0-2		15,644
10	Oct	2	(h)	Cardiff C	L	1-2	Ham	13,511
11		9	(a)	Portsmouth	D	1-1	McIlmoyle	12,749
12		16	(h)	Carlisle U	W	3-0	Lyall 2, Ingram	15,430
13		18	(a)	Orient	L	2-3	Ingram, McIlmoyle	7,391
14		23	(a)	Birmingham C	D	2-2	Ingram, Tarbuck	28,956
15		30	(h)	Hull C	W	3-1	Ingram 2, Clarke	14,413
16	Nov	6	(a)	Middlesbrough	W	1-0	Tarbuck	21,907
17		13	(h)	Sheffield W	W	1-0	Heppolette	16,903
18		20	(a)	Swindon T	D	1-1	Ingram	10,833
19		27	(h)	Watford	W	2-0	Spark, Tarbuck	11,318
20	Dec	4	(a)	Blackpool	D	1-1	Clarke	18,912
21		11	(h)	Millwall	W	4-0	Tarbuck, Ingram (pen), Clarke, Lyall	14,097
22		18	(a)	Oxford U	L	0-2		7,758
23		27	(h)	Bristol C	W	1-0	Lyall	19,738
24	Jan	1	(a)	Charlton Ath	L	1-2	Clark	8,038
25		8	(h)	Luton T	L	0-1		12,844
26		22	(a)	Norwich C	D	1-1	Bird	21,390
27		29	(h)	Orient	D	1-1	Ingram	19,692
28	Feb	12	(h)	Birmingham C	D	0-0		17,794
29		19	(a)	Hull C	L	2-3	Young, Tarbuck	14,313
30	Mar	4	(a)	Sheffield W	L	0-1		12,162
31		11	(h)	Portsmouth	W	4-0	McIlmoyle, Tarbuck, Lyall (pen), Young	10,575
32		18	(a)	Fulham	D	0-0		9,071
33		25	(h)	Q.P.R.	D	1-1	Tarbuck	12,304
34		29	(a)	Cardiff C	L	2-5	Tarbuck, Spavin	13,294
35	Apr	1	(a)	Bristol C	L	1-4	Tarbuck	12,962
36		4	(h)	Sunderland	L	1-3	Young	13,450
37		15	(a)	Watford	L	0-1		5,507
38		17	(h)	Middlesbrough	W	1-0	McIlmoyle	11,388
39		22	(h)	Blackpool	L	1-4	McIlmoyle	19,819
40		25	(a)	Burnley	L	0-1		13,020
41		29	(a)	Millwall	L	0-2		19,123
42	May	1	(h)	Swindon T	D	2-2	Lamb, Tarbuck	9,566

FINAL LEAGUE POSITION: 18th in Division Two

Appearances

Sub. Appearances

Goals

Kelly	Ross	McNab	Bird	Hawkins	Spavin	Heppolette	Ham	McIlmoyle	Spark	Clark	McMahon	Lyall	Wilson	Brown	Ritchie	Tarbuck	Ingram	Lamb	Connor	Young	Hughes	Blyth	Bruce	Williams	No.
1	2	3	4	5	6	7	8	9	10	11															1
1		3	4	5	6	7	8	9	10	11	2														2
1		3	4	5		7	8	9	6	11*	2	10	12												3
1		3	4	5	6	7	8	9	10		2		11												4
1		3*	4	5	6	11	8	9	10		2	12	7												5
			4	5	6	7	8	9	2	11		10		1	3										6
		3	4	5	6	7	8	9	2	11		10		1											7
		3	4	5	6	7	8	9	2	11		10		1											8
		3	4	5	6	7	8*	9		11	2	10		1		12									9
		3	4	5	6	7	8*	9		11	2	10		1			12								10
1		3*	4	5	6	7	8	9	12		2	10				11									11
1			4	5	6	7	9	10	2			8			3	11									12
1			4	5	6	7	8	9	2			10			3	11									13
1			4	5	6	7		9	12		2	10			3*	11	8								14
1			4	5	6	7		9		8	2	10			3	11									15
1			4	5	6	7		10			2	8			3	9	11								16
1			4	5*	6	7		9	12	8	2	10			3	11									17
1			4	5	6	7		9*	12	8	2	10			3	11									18
1			4	5	6	7*			12	10	2	8			3	9	11								19
1			4	5	6	7				8	2	10			3	9	11								20
1			4	5	6				7	8	2	10			3	9	11								21
1			4	5	6				7	8	2	10			3	9	11								22
1		3	4	5	6*			9	7	8	2	10				12	11								23
1		3	4	5		7		9		8	2	10				11		6							24
1		3	4	5		7		9		8	2	10	12			11*		6							25
1		3	4	5*	6	7		9		8	2	10				11	12								26
1		5	4		6	7		9			2	10				12	11	8*	3						27
1		5	4		6			9		8	2	10					11		3	7					28
1		3	4		6	7		5		10*						8	11	12	2	9					29
1		2	4	5	6	7		9				10					8		3	11					30
1		2	4	5	6	7		9				10					11		3	8					31
1		3	4	5	6			9	7			10					11		2	8					32
1		3	4	5	6	7*		9	12			10					11		2	8					33
1		3	4	5*	6	7		8				10					9		2	11	12				34
1		5	4		6	7		9			2					11		10	3	8*	12				35
1			4	5	6	7		9	12		2	10				11*			3	8					36
1			4	5	6			9	7		2	10				11			3	8					37
1		3	4	5*	6	7		9	12		2					11			10	8					38
1		3*	4	5	6	7		9	12		2					11			10	8					39
1			4	5		7		9	6*		2	8	12			11			3	10					40
1	3		4	5		7			6		2					9			11	10					41
	3		4	5		7*		9	6		2	12								10		1	8	11	42
36	3	25	42	38	36	36	13	35	19	19	32	34	2	5	12	19	18	7	14	14		1	1	1	
								8				2	3			4	1	2		2					
		1		1	2	4		10	1	5		6				10	8	1		3					

1972-73

1	Aug	12	(h)	Aston Villa	L	0-1		17,371
2		19	(a)	Luton T	L	0-1		11,507
3		26	(h)	Q.P.R.	D	1-1	Young	9,242
4		29	(a)	Burnley	L	0-2		13,166
5	Sep	2	(a)	Fulham	W	3-1	Young, Wilson 2	7,640
6		9	(h)	Hull C	W	1-0	Tarbuck	8,136
7		16	(a)	Portsmouth	W	1-0	Tarbuck	6,965
8		19	(a)	Middlesbrough	D	0-0		9,679
9		23	(h)	Carlisle U	W	1-0	Tarbuck	10,957
10		25	(h)	Orient	D	0-0		10,709
11		30	(a)	Oxford U	W	2-0	Young (pen), Wilson	8,850
12	Oct	7	(h)	Sheffield W	D	1-1	Wilson	15,600
13		14	(a)	Swindon T	L	2-3	Tarbuck, McNab	8,198
14		21	(h)	Millwall	W	1-0	Tarbuck	10,010
15		28	(a)	Cardiff C	L	0-3		12,208
16	Nov	3	(a)	Orient	W	2-1	Young, Bruce	5,661
17		11	(h)	Middlesbrough	L	0-1		10,015
18		18	(a)	Nottingham F	W	1-0	Bruce	10,382
19		25	(h)	Brighton	W	4-0	Bruce 2, Young (pen), McNab	8,005
20	Dec	2	(a)	Huddersfield T	D	0-0		6,900
21		9	(h)	Blackpool	L	0-3		18,822
22		16	(a)	Sunderland	D	0-0		11,529
23		23	(h)	Bristol C	D	3-3	McMahon, Bruce, Tarbuck	7,700
24		26	(a)	Carlisle U	L	1-6	Bruce	9,939
25		30	(h)	Luton T	W	2-0	Wilson, Bruce	9,638
26	Jan	6	(a)	Q.P.R.	L	0-3		10,519
27		20	(h)	Fulham	L	0-3		5,759
28		27	(a)	Hull C	L	2-6	Young, Spark	9,120
29	Feb	10	(h)	Portsmouth	L	0-5		6,230
30		17	(a)	Aston Villa	D	1-1	Bruce	27,717
31	Mar	3	(a)	Sheffield W	L	1-2	Tarbuck	13,427
32		10	(h)	Swindon T	D	1-1	Bruce	6,468
33		17	(a)	Millwall	L	1-4	Holden	8,233
34		19	(h)	Sunderland	L	1-3	Bruce	7,636
35		24	(h)	Cardiff C	D	0-0		6,889
36		31	(a)	Brighton	L	0-2		12,047
37	Apr	7	(h)	Huddersfield T	D	0-0		7,896
38		14	(a)	Blackpool	L	0-2		12,195
39		21	(h)	Nottingham F	W	2-1	Young (pen), Bruce	7,701
40		23	(a)	Bristol C	L	1-2	Bruce	10,799
41		24	(h)	Oxford U	L	0-1		7,792
42		28	(h)	Burnley	D	1-1	Bruce	21,550

FINAL LEAGUE POSITION: 19th in Division Two

Appearances

Sub. Appearances

Goals

Kelly	McMahon	McNab	Bird	Hawkins	Connor	Young	Lamb	McIlMoyle	Williams	Heppolette	Spark	Wilson	Tarbuck	Clark	Davies	Spavin	Bruce	Brown	Ross	Morley	Holden	Snookes	Baxter	No.
1	2	3	4	5	6	7	8	9	10	11														1
1	2	3	4	5	6*	10				7	12	8	9	11										2
1	2	3	4	5		10				7	6	8		11	9									3
1	2	3	4	5		10				7	8	12		11*	9	6								4
1	2	3	4	5		10*				7	8	11	9			6	12							5
1	2	3	4	5		10				11	8	7	9			6								6
1	2	3	4	5		10				7	8	11	9			6								7
1	2	3	4*	5		10				11	8	7	9			6	12							8
	2	3	4	5		10				11*	8	7	9			6	12	1						9
	2	3	4	5		10					8	7	9			6	11	1						10
	2	3	4	5		10				11	8	7	9			6		1						11
1	2	3*	4	5		10				11	8	7	9			6	12							12
1	2	3		5		10				11	4	8	9			6	7							13
1	2	3	4	5		10*				11	8	7	9			6	12							14
1	2	3	4	5		10*				11	8	7	9			6	12							15
1	2	3	4	5		10				11	8	7	9*			6	12							16
1	2	3	5			10		12		11*	4	7	9			6	8							17
1	2	3	4	5		10		9			8	7				6	11							18
1	2	3	4	5		10		9			8	7				6	11							19
1	2	3*	4	5				9			8	7	12	10		6	11							20
1	2		4	5	3	10*		9			8	7	12			6	11							21
1	2		4	5	3			9			8	7	10			6	11							22
1	2		4	5	3			9			8	7	10			6	11							23
1	2*	12	4	5	3			9			8	7	10			6	11							24
1		3	4	5	6			9			8	7	10				11							25
1		3	4	5	6			9			8	7*	10				11		2	12				26
1	2	3		5	10*	8		9			12	7				6	11		4					27
1		3	4	5		11					8	7				6	10		2		9			28
1	2	3	4	5		8		9			10	7*	12			6	11							29
		3	4	2	10	6		9			5	8	7				11	1						30
		3	2	5	6	8		9			4	11	10				7	1						31
		4	3	2	6	7		9			5	11	10				8	1						32
		3	4	6	2	8		9			5	7	10				11*	1		12				33
		3*	4	5	2	7		9			12	11					8	1		6	10			34
	2		4	5	3	7		9			12	11*					8	1		6	10			35
	2		4	5	8*				10	11	7						6	1	12		9	3		36
1	2		4	5		11	7	10			8						6				9	3		37
1	2		4	5		11	7	9*			8						6		12		10	3		38
	2		4	5		11	7	9*			8	10					6	1	12			3		39
	2		4	5		11	8	9			6	7*					10	1				3	12	40
1	2		4	8		11	7	9			6						10					3	5	41
1	2		4	5	7	11	8				10						9					3	6	42
30	36	30	41	39	15	29	14	24	2	17	36	33	23	7	2	24	28	12	3	2	6	7	2	
	1						1				3	2	2	1			7		2	2	1		1	
	1	2				7					1	5	7				13				1			

15

1973-74

No	Month	Date		Opponent	Result	Score	Scorers	Attendance
1	Aug	25	(a)	Aston Villa	L	0-2		28,861
2	Sep	1	(h)	Swindon T	D	1-1	Bruce	12,034
3		8	(a)	Hull C	L	0-1		7,009
4		11	(h)	Millwall	W	2-0	Burns, Holden	10,325
5		15	(h)	Bristol C	D	1-1	Young	10,790
6		18	(a)	West Brom A	W	2-0	Holden, Bruce	11,822
7		22	(a)	Nottingham F	D	1-1	Burns	12,598
8		29	(h)	Portsmouth	W	2-1	Baxter, Bruce	10,640
9	Oct	1	(h)	West Brom A	W	3-1	Burns, Young, McMahon	15,419
10		6	(a)	Fulham	D	0-0		10,520
11		13	(h)	Sunderland	W	1-0	Young (pen)	21,747
12		20	(a)	Notts Co	L	1-2	Williams	12,479
13		22	(a)	Millwall	L	1-5	Burns	7,625
14		27	(h)	Cardiff C	D	2-2	Spark, Bruce	12,050
15	Nov	3	(a)	Orient	D	2-2	Bruce 2	12,484
16		10	(h)	Blackpool	L	1-3	Bruce	21,580
17		17	(a)	Oxford U	D	1-1	Bruce	6,750
18		24	(h)	Luton T	D	2-2	Young 2	10,279
19	Dec	8	(h)	Bolton W	W	2-0	Young, Bruce	14,715
20		11	(a)	Middlesbrough	L	0-3		23,980
21		15	(h)	Crystal Palace	D	1-1	Sadler	9,121
22		22	(a)	Portsmouth	L	0-3		13,957
23		26	(h)	Carlisle U	L	0-1		11,446
24		29	(h)	Hull C	W	2-0	Holden 2	10,050
25	Jan	1	(a)	Swindon T	L	1-3	Williams	8,299
26		12	(a)	Bristol C	D	0-0		11,450
27		19	(h)	Aston Villa	D	0-0		10,766
28	Feb	3	(a)	Crystal Palace	L	0-2		24,575
29		10	(h)	Nottingham F	W	2-1	Richardson (og), Bird	13,486
30		16	(a)	Sunderland	L	1-2	Stiles	21,129
31		23	(h)	Fulham	L	0-1		9,412
32	Mar	2	(a)	Carlisle U	D	2-2	Elwiss 2	7,671
33		9	(a)	Cardiff C	L	0-2		7,216
34		16	(h)	Notts Co	L	0-2		8,907
35		23	(a)	Blackpool	L	0-3		13,243
36		30	(h)	Orient	L	0-1		7,650
37	Apr	6	(a)	Luton T	L	2-4	Burns, Sadler	11,806
38		12	(h)	Sheffield W	D	0-0		11,286
39		13	(h)	Oxford U	D	0-0		7,707
40		15	(a)	Sheffield W	L	0-1		17,332
41		20	(a)	Bolton W	W	2-0	Bird, Elwiss	17,273
42		27	(h)	Middlesbrough	L	2-4	Elwiss 2	16,177

FINAL LEAGUE POSITION: 21st in Division Two

Appearances

Sub. Appearances

Goals

Kelly	McMahon	McNab	Burns	Hawlins	Spark	Morley	Spavin	Wilson	Holden	Young	Baxter	Stiles	Bruce	Bird	Lamb	Brown	Williams	Coleman	Snookes	Sadler	Carrick	Hudson	Healey	Treacy	Elwiss	Smith			
1	2	3*	4	5	6	7	8	9	10	11	12																		1
1	2	3	8	5		7			10	9*	12	4		6	11														2
1	2	3	9	5			8*		10		4		6	11	7	12													3
1	2	3	7	5					8	9		4	6	11	10														4
1	2	3	8*	5		12			9	11	4	7	10		6														5
	2	3	10	5					9	11	4	6	8		7	1													6
	2	3	10	5					9	11	4	6	8		7	1													7
	2	3	10	5					9*	11	4	7	8		6	1	12												8
	2	3*	10	5	7					11	4	6	8			1	12	9											9
	2	3	9	5	4*					11	6	7	10			1	12	8											10
	2	3	8	5	4				10		6	7				1	11	9											11
	2	3	10	5	12				8	4	6*	7				1	11	9											12
	2	3	10	5	6	12			9	4		7				1	11		8*										13
	2	3	8		6	12			10	11	4	7		5		1			9*										14
	2		10		6	8			9	11	4	7		5		1				3									15
	2		8	5	6				9	11	12	7*	10			1				3	4								16
	2		9	5*	7					11		6	10	4		1				3	8	12							17
	2		10		8					11		6*	9	5	7	1				3	4	12							18
	2	3	8		4					11		7	9	5	10					6		1							19
	2	3*	10	12						11		6	9	5	7					4			1	8					20
	2		8	5						11		7*	9	4			12			3	6		1	10					21
	2		8	5					10	11		4	9	6						3	7		1						22
	2		10	5					9			6	8	4			11			3	7		1						23
	2		10	5					9			8	4				11			3	6		1	7					24
	2		10	5					9		12	8	4				11*			3	6		1	7					25
	2	3	8	7					9			4	10	6		1				5			11						26
	2	3*	8	10		12			7			6	11	4		1				5			9						27
	2		10	8					9			5	6	7	1				3	4			11						28
	2		10	4					9*			5	6	7	1		12			3	8		11						29
	2		10						9			5	4	8	7	1				3	6		11						30
	2		10			12						5	8	4	7*	1		9		3	6		11						31
	2	3	9									6	7	4	8	1				5			11	10					32
	2	3	8		12	9						6	4	7*	1					5			11	10					33
	2	3	8	5*	7				12	11			6			1				4			10	9					34
	2	3*	8		7				12	11		6	4			1				5			9	10					35
	2	3	8							11		4	6	7		1				5			9	10					36
	2		8	6	3							5	4			7	1			11			12	9		10*			37
	2		8	5	3				10			4	6	7		1				11			9						38
	2		8	5	3				9*			6	4			1				11			7	10	12				39
	2		8	5	3							4	6	7*		1				11			10	9	12				40
	2		8	5	3	7						4	6			1				9			11	10					41
	2		8	5	6	7						4	3			1				11			9	10					42
5	42	23	42	31	17	7	4	1	21	24	24	27	26	28	19	30	6	7	13	27	1	6	19	11	1				
		1	2	3	2				2	1	3				1		5				2			1		2			
	1		5		1				4	6	1	1	9	2			2			2				5					

1974-75

1	Aug	17	(h)	Plymouth Argyle	W	1-0	Morley	11,663
2		24	(a)	Watford	L	2-3	Elwiss, Holden	8,918
3		31	(h)	Walsall	W	3-2	Elwiss, Charlton, Morley	7,446
4	Sep	3	(h)	Bury	W	3-0	Charlton, Holden 2	10,404
5		7	(a)	Aldershot	W	2-1	Morley, Holden	6,357
6		14	(h)	Blackburn R	D	0-0		18,042
7		17	(h)	Charlton Ath	W	2-0	Elwiss, Morley	11,869
8		21	(a)	Peterborough U	D	0-0		13,120
9		24	(a)	Crystal Palace	L	0-1		19,680
10		28	(h)	Bournemouth	W	5-2	Lamb, Burns, Charlton (pen), Elwiss, Holden	10,421
11	Oct	1	(a)	Bury	L	0-2		11,914
12		5	(a)	Hereford U	D	2-2	Holden, Bird	11,488
13		12	(h)	Colchester U	L	0-2		10,259
14		19	(a)	Brighton & HA	W	4-0	Holden 2, Elwiss, Morley	16,413
15		22	(h)	Gillingham	W	1-0	Bird	9,867
16		26	(h)	Grimsby T	W	2-0	Charlton (pen), Morley	9,934
17	Nov	2	(a)	Halifax T	L	0-3		4,878
18		6	(a)	Gillingham	L	1-2	Shipperley (og)	10,494
19		9	(h)	Southend U	L	1-4	Elwiss	8,295
20		15	(a)	Tranmere R	L	1-3	Holden	6,534
21		30	(h)	Huddersfield T	W	4-0	Elwiss, Holden 2, Charlton	7,958
22	Dec	7	(a)	Wrexham	L	1-2	Holden	8,226
23		21	(h)	Port Vale	W	1-0	Bird	8,743
24		26	(a)	Blackburn R	L	0-3		24,005
25		28	(h)	Chesterfield	W	2-1	Darling (og), Charlton	9,258
26	Jan	11	(h)	Wrexham	W	3-1	Elwiss, Morley (pen), Holden	9,293
27		18	(a)	Huddersfield T	W	1-0	Charlton	7,654
28	Feb	1	(a)	Southend U	D	1-1	Holden	9,134
29		8	(h)	Halifax T	W	1-0	Holden	9,786
30		15	(a)	Swindon T	L	0-1		11,892
31		18	(h)	Swindon T	W	2-0	Elwiss, Morley	11,139
32		22	(h)	Tranmere R	W	1-0	Holden	10,798
33		28	(a)	Walsall	L	0-2		10,151
34	Mar	8	(h)	Crystal Palace	D	1-1	Coleman	12,119
35		15	(a)	Bournemouth	L	0-1		7,337
36		18	(a)	Plymouth Argyle	L	1-2	Charlton	22,063
37		22	(h)	Aldershot	W	3-1	Holden, Bird, McMahon	7,474
38		29	(a)	Port Vale	L	1-2	Tartt (og)	6,583
39		31	(a)	Chesterfield	D	0-0		8,705
40	Apr	1	(h)	Peterbrough U	D	1-1	Bird	6,507
41		5	(a)	Grimsby T	L	1-2	Elwiss	6,221
42		12	(h)	Hereford U	D	2-2	Burns, Morley (pen)	6,528
43		19	(a)	Colchester U	D	2-2	Smith, Morley	5,228
44		22	(h)	Watford U	D	2-2	Burns, Bird	5,819
45		26	(h)	Brighton & HA	W	1-0	Winstanley (og)	6,222
46		29	(a)	Charlton Ath	L	1-3	Coleman	24,165

FINAL LEAGUE POSITION: 9th in Division Three

Appearances

Sub. Appearances

Goals

18

Brown	McMahon	Spark	Charlton	Bird	Sadler	Lamb	Morley	Elwiss	Coleman	Burns	Smith	Holden	Baxter	Fielding	Williams	Treacy	Stiles	Tunks	Doyle	Thomson	Lawrenson	No.
1	2	3	4	5	6	7	8	9	10*	11	12											1
1	2	3	4	5	6	7	10	8		11		9*	12									2
1	2	3	4	6	5	7	8	10		11		9										3
1	2	3	4	5	6	7	8	9		11		10										4
1	2	3	4	5		7	8	9		11		10	6									5
1	2	3	11	6	5	7	8	10		4		9										6
1	2	3	11	5	6	7	8	9		4		10										7
1	2	3	11	5	6	7	8	9		4		10										8
1	2	3	11	5	6	7	8	9		4		10										9
1	2	3	11*	5	6	7	8	9	12	4		10										10
1		3	11	5	6	7	8	9		4		10	2									11
1	2		4	5	6	7	8	9		3		10	12		11*							12
1			4	5	6	7	8	9		3		10	2		11*	12						13
1	2		4	5	6	7	8	9		3		10				11						14
1	2	11		5	6	7	8	9		3		10				4						15
1	2		4	5	6	7	8	9		3		10				11						16
1	2		4	5	6	7	8*	9		3		10				11	12					17
1	2	11		5	6	7	8	10		3		9*				4	12					18
1	2	11		5	6	7	8	9		3		10				4						19
		3	11	5	6*	7	8	9				10	2			12		1	4			20
			11	5	6	7	12	9		3		10	2				8*	1	4			21
			11	5	6	7	8	9		3		10	2					1	4			22
			11	4	5	7	8	9		3		10	2				6	1				23
			11	5	6	7	8	9		3		10	2				4	1				24
			11	5	6	7	8	9		3		10	2				4	1				25
	2	4	11	5	6		8	9		3		10					7	1				26
	2	7	11	5	6		8	9		3		10					4	1				27
	2	4	11	5	6		8	9		3		10					7*	1	12			28
	2	4	11	5	6		8	9		3		10					7	1				29
	2	4	11	5	6*		8	9	12	3		10					7	1				30
	2	6	11	5			8	9	7	3		10					4	1				31
	2	6	11	5			8	9	7	3		10					4	1				32
	2	6	11	5			8*		7	3		10	12			9	4	1				33
	2	6	11	5			10		7	3		9	4				8	1				34
	3	6	11	5			10*	9	12	2		8					4	1	7			35
	2	6	11	5				9	8	3	12	10	7*				4	1				36
	2	6	11	5			8	9		3	7	10						1	4			37
	2	6	11	5			8	9	12	3	7	10*						1	4			38
	2	6		5			11	9	8			10		3				1	4	7		39
	2*	6		5			11	9	12	8		10		3			4	1		7		40
		2*		5			8	9	11	10	12			3	4		6	1		7		41
		6*		5			10	9	12	8		11	2	3				1	7	4		42
				5			11	9	12	8		10	6	2	3			1	4	7*		43
				5			11	12	10	8			6	3	9			1	4	7*	2	44
				5			11	9	7	8		10*	6	3				1	4	12	2	45
				5			11	9	7	8		10	6	3				1	4		2	46
19	25	36	38	46	29	25	44	43	10	45	3	42	9	9	10	8	17	27	12	6	3	
							1	1	7		3		3				2	2	1	1		
	1			8	6	1	10	10	2	3	1	17										

19

1975-76

								Scorers	Attendance
1	Aug	16	(h)	Colchester U	W	2-1	Treacy 2		6,324
2		23	(a)	Port Vale	D	1-1	Treacy		4,282
3		30	(h)	Millwall	W	2-1	Elwiss, Treacy		7,707
4	Sep	6	(a)	Gillingham	L	0-1			5,786
5		13	(h)	Walsall	W	3-1	Elwiss, Bruce, Treacy		7,015
6		20	(a)	Aldershot	D	1-1	Bruce		3,883
7		22	(a)	Southend U	W	2-0	Morley, Coleman		4,583
8		27	(h)	Cardiff C	W	3-1	Elwiss, Treacy, Morley (pen)		8,103
9	Oct	4	(a)	Chesterfield	L	0-3			4,000
10		11	(a)	Brighton & HA	L	0-1			14,375
11		18	(h)	Crystal Palace	D	0-0			10,971
12		21	(h)	Peterborough U	W	2-1	Treacy, Bruce		9,597
13		25	(a)	Mansfield T	W	1-0	Elwiss		6,677
14	Nov	1	(h)	Hereford U	L	3-4	Baxter, Morley (pen), Treacy		9,682
15		4	(a)	Halifax T	L	1-2	Morley		3,366
16		8	(a)	Swindon T	W	3-1	Bruce, Elwiss, Taylor (og)		6,332
17		15	(h)	Bury	D	0-0			11,017
18		29	(a)	Grimsby T	D	0-0			4,519
19	Dec	6	(h)	Wrexham	L	0-1			7,438
20		20	(a)	Sheffield W	D	2-2	Smith, Elwiss		8,553
21		27	(a)	Chester	L	0-3			8,137
22	Jan	10	(a)	Millwall	L	0-2			6,057
23		13	(h)	Rotherham U	W	3-2	Morley, Smith, Elwiss		6,289
24		17	(h)	Aldershot	W	1-0	Earls (og)		6,198
25		24	(a)	Walsall	L	1-3	Treacy		6,721
26		31	(a)	Peterborough U	L	0-2			7,728
27	Feb	3	(h)	Shrewsbury T	L	0-2			4,995
28		7	(h)	Halifax T	W	2-1	Elwiss, Dolye		5,480
29		14	(h)	Swindon T	W	4-2	Bruce, Treacy, Brown (pen), Smith		5,868
30		21	(a)	Bury	L	0-2			7,049
31		24	(h)	Southend U	W	5-1	Smith 2, Treacy, Elwiss 2		5,210
32		28	(h)	Mansfield T	L	0-2			6,945
33	Mar	9	(h)	Chesterfield	W	3-1	Elwiss, Bruce 2		4,621
34		13	(h)	Brighton & HA	W	1-0	Bruce (pen)		6,720
35		16	(a)	Crystal Palace	L	0-2			22,213
36		20	(h)	Grimsby T	D	0-0			6,586
37		27	(a)	Wrexham	W	2-1	Smith, Bruce		4,906
38		30	(h)	Sheffield W	W	4-2	Elwiss, McMahon, Bruce 2		6,899
39	Apr	3	(a)	Colchester U	D	1-1	Elwiss		2,657
40		7	(a)	Cardiff C	L	0-1			12,447
41		10	(h)	Gillingham	W	4-0	McMahon, Bruce 2 (1 pen), Smith		6,349
42		17	(a)	Shrewsbury T	L	0-1			3,547
43		19	(h)	Chester	D	0-0			6,719
44		20	(a)	Rotherham U	D	1-1	Coleman		4,874
45		24	(h)	Port Vale	W	3-0	Elwiss, Bruce 2		5,783
46		28	(a)	Hereford U	L	1-3	Elwiss		7,592

FINAL LEAGUE POSITION: 8th in Division Three

Appearances

Sub. Appearances

Goals

20

Tunks	McMahon	Williams	Doyle	Bird	Spark	Lamb	Burns	Treacy	Elwiss	Morley	Baxter	Sadler	Bruce	Coleman	Taylor	Brown	Thompson	Smith	Lawrenson	Clarke	Robinson	Cameron	#
1	2	3	4	5	6	7	8	9	10	11													1
1	2	3		5	6	7	11	9	10	8	4												2
1	2	3	4		6	7	8	9	10	11	5												3
1	2	3	7*		5		8	9	10	11	6	4	12										4
1	2	3			6	4	8	9	10	11	5		7										5
1	2	3			6	4	8	9	10	11	5		7										6
1	2	3			6	4*	8	9	10	11	5		7	12									7
1	2	3			6		8	9	10	11	5	12	7	4*									8
1		3			6		8	9	10	11	5	2	7	12	4*								9
1		3			6		7	11	9	10*	5	2	8			4	12						10
1	2	3			6		8	11	9	10	5		7			4							11
1	2	3			6		8	9	10	11	5		7			4							12
1	2	3			6		8	9	10	11	5		7			4							13
1	2	3			6		8	9	10	11	5		7*			4		12					14
1	2	3			6		8	9	10	11	5		7			4							15
1	2	3			6		8	9	10	11		5	7			4							16
1	2	3			6		7	9	10	11		5	8			4							17
1	2	3			6		7	9	10	11		5	8			4							18
1		3			6		7	9*	10	11	5		8	12		4		2					19
1	2	3	8		6	7			10	11	4	5						9					20
	2	3	4		6		8	9	10		5					7		11		1			21
	2*	3	4		10			9		11	5		8	12		7			6	1			22
	2	3					8	9	10	11	5		12	6*		7		4		1			23
1	2	3	4				8	9	10	11	5			6		7							24
1	2	3			6		8	9	10		5		11			7		4					25
1	2	3			6		7		10	11	5		8			4		9					26
1		3			6		8*	12	10		5		11	7		4		9	2				27
1	2	3	4		6			9	10			5	8			11		7					28
1	2	3	4					9	10			5	8			11		7	6				29
1	2	3	4					9	10			5	11			8		7	6				30
1	2	3	4					9	10			5	7			8		11	6				31
1	2	3	4*					9	10			5	7	12		8		11	6				32
1	2	3	4						10			5	11	8		7		9	6				33
1	2	3	4						10			5	8	7		11		9	6				34
1	2	3	4						10			5	11	8		7		9	6				35
1	2	3	4					9				5	11	7		8		10	6				36
1	2	3	4		12			9				5	11	7		10		8	6*				37
1	2	3	4						10			5	11	8		7		9	6				38
1	2*	3	4		12			9				5	8	7		11		10	6				39
1			4		6			10		12		5	11	2		7		9	3		8*		40
1	2*	6	4		12			10				5	11	8		7		9	3				41
1	2		4		3			9				5	11	8		7		10	6				42
1	2	3	4						10			5	11	8		7*		9	6			12	43
1	2	3	4			7			10			5	11	8				9	6				44
1	2	3	4					9				5	11	7		10		8	6				45
1	2	3	4				8		10			5	11	7*				9	6			12	46
43	41	44	24	2	29	8	27	27	46	25	21	28	38	15	3	29	1	27	24	3	1		
			3				1				1	1	2	5			1	1			1	1		
	2		1				11	15	5	1			15	2		1		7					

21

1976-77

1	Aug	21	(a)	Mansfield T	L	1-3	Elwiss	5,688
2		28	(h)	Brighton & HA	D	1-1	Mitchell	6,265
3	Sep	4	(a)	Oxford U	D	2-2	Elwiss 2	4,397
4		11	(a)	Chester	D	0-0		4,151
5		14	(h)	Port Vale	W	4-0	Bruce 3 (1 pen), Coleman	6,586
6		18	(h)	Rotherham U	D	0-0		7,899
7		25	(a)	Grimsby T	L	0-1		3,896
8	Oct	2	(h)	York C	W	4-2	Bruce, Burns, Elwiss 2	6,380
9		8	(a)	Tranmere R	D	0-0		5,005
10		12	(h)	Peterborough U	W	6-2	Bruce 2, Mitchell, Turner (og), Elwiss, Smith	5,651
11		16	(h)	Crystal Palace	W	2-1	Elwiss 2	10,524
12		23	(a)	Bury	L	2-3	Bruce 2	8,724
13		30	(a)	Gillingham	D	1-1	Bruce	5,070
14	Nov	1	(a)	Port Vale	D	0-0		4,686
15		16	(h)	Northampton T	W	3-0	Elwiss, Coleman, Tucker (og)	7,306
16		13	(a)	Reading	W	2-0	Elwiss, Bruce	6,612
17		27	(h)	Lincoln C	W	3-0	Bruce 2, Elwiss	7,964
18	Dec	4	(a)	Portsmouth	D	0-0		9,243
19		17	(h)	Shrewsbury T	W	2-1	Lawrenson, Sadler	7,809
20		27	(a)	Walsall	W	1-0	Bruce	8,769
21	Jan	1	(a)	Northampton T	W	1-0	Bruce	5,024
22		15	(a)	Peterborough U	D	0-0		5,308
23		22	(h)	Mansfield T	L	1-2	Elwiss	8,500
24		29	(a)	Chesterfield	D	1-1	Bruce	5,002
25	Feb	5	(a)	Brighton & H.A.	L	0-2		21,338
26		8	(h)	Swindon T	W	2-0	Bruce, Brown	9,409
27		12	(h)	Oxford U	W	2-1	Bruce, Elwiss	9,950
28		19	(h)	Chester	L	3-4	Elwiss 2, Bruce	10,101
29		26	(a)	Rotherham U	L	0-2		8,861
30	Mar	5	(h)	Grimsby T	W	2-1	Brown, Bruce	7,278
31		12	(a)	York C	W	2-0	Smith, Elwiss	3,575
32		15	(h)	Wrexham	W	2-1	Bruce 2	10,491
33		19	(h)	Tranmere R	W	1-0	Coleman	9,100
34		22	(a)	Crystal Palace	L	0-1		14,993
35		29	(h)	Sheffield W	W	4-1	Smith, Lawrenson, Elwiss, Bruce	11,753
36	Apr	2	(h)	Bury	L	0-1		9,795
37		9	(a)	Wrexham	L	0-2		10,545
38		11	(h)	Walsall	L	0-1		7,850
39		16	(a)	Sheffield W	L	0-1		13,217
40		19	(h)	Chesterfield	D	2-2	Thompson, Baxter	5,288
41		23	(h)	Reading	W	3-0	Thompson 2, Bruce	4,879
42		26	(h)	Gillingham	W	1-0	Elwiss	4,943
43		30	(a)	Lincoln C	L	0-2		5,357
44	May	3	(a)	Swindon	W	1-0	Elwiss	4,142
45		7	(h)	Portsmouth	D	0-0		5,347
46		14	(a)	Shrewsbury T	W	2-1	Bruce, Cochrane	2,849

FINAL LEAGUE POSITION: 6th in Division Three

Appearances

Sub. Appearances

Goals

Smith	Cameron	Williams	Doyle	Sadler	Lawrenson	Coleman	Lamb	Smith J	Elwiss	Bruce	Mitchell	Tunks	Brown	Burns	McMahon	Baxter	Thomson	Cochrane	#
1	2*	3	4	5	6	7	8	9	10	11	12								1
		3		5	6	2	4	9*	10	7	12	1	8	11					2
		3		5	6	7		9*	10	11	12	1	8	4	2				3
		3		5	6	7		9	10	11		1	8	4	2				4
		3		5	6	7	12	9*	10	11		1	8	4	2				5
		3	12	5	6	7	8*		10	9		1	11	4	2				6
	12	3	4		6				10	9	7	1	8	11	2*	5			7
		3	4		6	2			10	11	9	1	8	7		5			8
		3	7	5	6	2			10	11	9	1	8	4					9
		3	7	5	6	2	12		10	11	9*	1	8	4					10
		3		5	6	7		9	10	11		1	8	4	2				11
		3		5	6	7		9	10	11		1	8	4	2				12
		3	8	5	6	7		9	10	11		1		4	2				13
	3		8		6	7		9	10	11		1		4	2	5			14
		3	7	5	6	8		9	10	11		1		4	2				15
	3		8	5	6	7		9	10	11		1		4	2				16
		3		5	6	7		9	10	11		1	8	4	2				17
		3		5	6	7		9	10	11		1	8	4	2				18
		3		5	6	7		9	10	11		1	8	4	2				19
		3			6	7		9	10	11		1	8	4	2	5			20
		3		5	6	7		9	10	11		1	8	4	2				21
		3			6	7		9	10	11		1	8	4	2	5			22
		3			6	7		9	10	11		1	8	4	2	5			23
		3			6	7		9	10	11		1	8	4	2	5			24
	7*	3	12		6			9	10	11		1	8	4	2	5			25
		3			6	7			10	11	9	1	8	4	2	5			26
		3			6	7			10	11	9	1	8	4	2	5			27
		3			6	7			10	11	9	1	8	4	2	5			28
		3			6	7		9	10	11		1	8	4	2	5			29
		3	12		6	7		9	10	11		1	8	4*	2	5			30
	2	3	12		6	7		9	10	11*		1	8	4		5			31
	2	3			6	7		9	10	11		1	8	4		5			32
	2	3			6	7		9	10	11		1	8	4		5			33
	2	3			6	7		9	10	11		1	8	4		5			34
	2	3		5	6	7		9	10	11		1	8	4					35
1	2	3		5	6	7		9	10	11			8	4					36
1	2*	3		5	6	7		9	10	11			8	4	12				37
1		3	8		6	7		9	10	11				4	2	5			38
1		3	8		6	7		9*	10	11				4	2	5	12		39
1		3	8		6	7			10	11				4	2	5	9		40
1		3	8		6	7			10	11				4	2	5	9		41
1		3	8		6	7			10	11				4	2	5	9		42
		3	8		6	7			10	11	12	1		4	2	5	9*		43
	2	3	8		6	7		9*	10	11		1		4		5	12		44
	2	3	8		6	7		9	10	11		1		4*		5	12		45
	2	3	8		6	7			10	11		1		4				9	46
8	14	44	18	20	46	44	3	34	45	46	7	38	33	44	31	26	4	1	
	1		4				1	1			4				1		3		
3			1	2	3			19	24	2		2	1			1	3	1	

23

1977-78

1	Aug	20	(a)	Plymouth Argyle	D	0-0		7,154
2		27	(h)	Rotherham U	W	3-2	Thomson, Doyle, Bruce	5,964
3	Sep	3	(a)	Oxford U	L	0-1		4,804
4		10	(a)	Carlisle U	L	1-3	Bruce	5,743
5		13	(h)	Swindon T	D	1-1	Robinson	6,014
6		17	(h)	Hereford U	D	0-0		5,447
7		24	(a)	Colchester U	D	0-0		4,978
8		27	(a)	Walsall	D	0-0		5,138
9	Oct	1	(h)	Cambridge U	W	2-0	Bruce, Baxter	5,319
10		4	(h)	Sheffield W	W	2-1	Elwiss, Cross	7,627
11		8	(a)	Bradford C	D	1-1	Smith	5,815
12		15	(h)	Gillingham	W	2-0	Elwiss, Smith	7,212
13		22	(a)	Exeter C	L	0-2		5,444
14		25	(h)	Tranmere R	W	2-1	Baxter, Elwiss	7,906
15		29	(h)	Chester	W	2-1	Bruce 2	7,550
16	Nov	5	(a)	Port Vale	D	0-0		4,208
17		12	(h)	Wrexham	L	1-3	Bruce	10,342
18		19	(a)	Lincoln C	D	2-2	Bruce 2	3,924
19	Dec	3	(h)	Portsmouth	W	3-1	Bruce, Elwiss, Smith	5,936
20		10	(a)	Shrewsbury T	D	0-0		3,764
21		26	(h)	Bury	W	4-0	Bruce 2 (1 pen), Elwiss, Coleman	10,297
22		27	(h)	Chesterfield	W	1-0	Bruce	6,484
23		31	(a)	Peterborough U	L	0-1		7,134
24	Jan	2	(h)	Port Vale	W	2-0	Thomson, Bruce	10,930
25		6	(a)	Tranmere R	L	0-1		7,250
26		14	(h)	Plymouth Argyle	W	5-2	Baxter, Bruce, Coleman, Thomson, Elwiss	6,500
27	Feb	4	(h)	Carlisle U	W	2-1	Bruce (2 pen)	9,095
28		11	(a)	Hereford U	D	0-0		4,791
29		21	(h)	Oxford U	W	3-2	Thomson 2, Bruce	6,189
30		25	(a)	Cambridge U	D	1-1	Thomson	5,766
31		28	(h)	Colchester U	W	4-0	Bruce 4 (2 pen)	9,225
32	Mar	4	(h)	Bradford C	W	3-1	McMahon, Elwiss 2	11,920
33		7	(a)	Swindon T	W	2-0	Baxter, Bruce	10,211
34		11	(a)	Gillingham	L	1-2	Coleman	9,568
35		18	(h)	Exeter C	D	0-0		9,189
36		24	(a)	Chester	W	2-1	Bruce, Elwiss	7,864
37		25	(h)	Chesterfield	D	0-0		10,922
38		27	(a)	Bury	D	1-1	Thomson	9,783
39	Apr	1	(h)	Peterborough U	L	0-1		9,695
40		4	(h)	Walsall	W	1-0	Paul (og)	11,239
41		8	(a)	Wrexham	D	0-0		19,008
42		15	(h)	Lincoln C	W	4-0	Robinson, Baxter, Bruce, Coleman	11,208
43		18	(a)	Sheffield W	L	0-1		12,426
44		22	(a)	Portsmouth	W	2-0	Bruce, Elwiss	6,866
45		25	(a)	Rotherham U	L	1-2	Bruce	6,646
46		29	(h)	Shrewsbury T	D	2-2	Elwiss, Bruce	16,078

FINAL LEAGUE POSITION: 3rd in Division Three

Appearances

Sub. Appearances

Goals

Tunks	McMahon	Wilson	Doyle	Baxter	Cross	Coleman	Brown	Thomson	Elwiss	Bruce	Burns	Cameron	Smith	Robinson	Haslegrave	Uzelac	Spavin	
1	2	3	4*	5	6	7	8	9	10	11	12							1
1	2	3	4	5	6		8	9	10	11	7							2
1		3	4	5	6	7		9*	10	11	8	2	12					3
1	2	3	4	5	6	7		9	10	11	8							4
1	2	3	4	5	6	7		9	10	11	8*			12				5
1	2	3	4	5	6	7		12	10	11	8*			9				6
1	2	3	4	5	6	7			10	11	8	9						7
1		3	4	5	6	7			10	11	8	2	9					8
1		3	4	5	6	7			10	11		2	9		8			9
1		3	4	5	6	7			10	11		2	9		8			10
1		3	4	5	6	7			10	11		2	9		8			11
1		3	4	5	6	7			10	11*		2	9	12	8			12
1		3	4	5	6	7		9*	10		12	2	11		8			13
1		3	4	5	6	7			10	11		2	9		8			14
1		3	4	5	6	7			10	11		2	9		8			15
1		3	4	5		7			10	11		2	9		8	6		16
1		3	4	5		7			10	11		2	9*		8	5	12	17
1	3*	4	5			7			10	11	6	2	9		8		12	18
1	2		4	5		7			10	11	6	3	9		8			19
1	2		4	5		7			10	11	6	3	9		8			20
1	2			5	6	7		9	10	11	4*	3			8		12	21
1	2			5	6	7		9	10	11	4	3			8			22
1	2			5	6	7		9	10	11	4	3			8			23
1	2			5	6	7		9	10	11	4	3			8			24
1	2			5	6	7		9	10	11	4	3			8			25
1	2	12		5	6*	7		9	10	11	4	3			8			26
1	2			5	6	7		9	10	11	4	3			8			27
1		7		5	6	2		9	10	11	4	3			8			28
1		7		5	6	2		9	10	11	4	3			8			29
1		4		5	6	2		9	10	11	7	3			8			30
1		7		5	6	2		9	10	11	4	3			8			31
1	2			5	6	7		9	10	11	4	3			8			32
1	2			5	6	7		9	10	11	4	3			8			33
1	2			5	6	7		9	10	11	4	3			8			34
1	2			5	6	7		9*	10	11	4	3			8		12	35
1	2			5	6	7		9	10	11	4	3			8			36
1	2	12		5*	6	7		9	10	11	4	3			8			37
1	2	5			6			9	10	11	4	3			8	7		38
1	2*	12		5	6	7		9	10	11	4	3			8			39
1	2			5	6	7			10	11	4	3		9	8			40
1	2			5	6	7			10	11	4	3		9	8			41
1	2	12		5	6	7			10	11	4*	3		9	8			42
1	2*	12		5	6	7			10	11	4	3		9	8			43
1	2			5	6	7			10	11	4	3		9	8			44
1	2	12		5	6*	7			10	11	4	3		9	8			45
1	2	12		5	6	7			10	11	4	3		9*	8			46
46	30	18	25	45	40	45	2	25	46	45	36	40	14	8	38	2	1	
			7				1				2		1	2			1	
	1		1	5	1	4		7	11	27			3	2				

25

1978-79

1	Aug	19	(a)	Cardiff C	D	2-2	Bruce 2	7,812
2		22	(h)	Blackburn R	W	4-1	Robinson, Doyle, Bruce 2	15,412
3		26	(h)	Sheffield U	D	2-2	Robinson 2	13,208
4	Sep	2	(a)	Sunderland	L	1-3	Robinson	16,819
5		9	(h)	Millwall	D	0-0		8,926
6		16	(a)	Oldham Ath	L	0-2		9,766
7		23	(h)	Stoke C	L	0-1		14,057
8		30	(a)	Brighton & HA	L	1-5	Cochrane	19,217
9	Oct	7	(a)	Cambridge U	L	0-1		5,398
10		14	(h)	Crystal Palace	L	2-3	Haslegrave, Thomson	10,795
11		21	(a)	Fulham	L	3-5	Bruce, Baxter, Coleman	8,719
12		28	(h)	Burnley	D	2-2	Thomson, Bruce	15,014
13	Nov	4	(a)	West Ham U	L	1-3	Thomson	23,579
14		11	(h)	Cardiff C	W	2-1	Robinson 2	9,268
15		18	(a)	Sheffield U	W	1-0	Bruce	14,807
16		21	(h)	Sunderland	W	3-1	Thomson, Robinson, Bruce	13,204
17		25	(a)	Orient	L	0-2		4,702
18	Dec	9	(a)	Luton T	W	2-1	Robinson (pen), Baxter	7,036
19		12	(h)	Charlton Ath	W	6-1	Coleman, Potts 2, Bruce 2, Robinson	8,500
20		16	(h)	Notts Co	D	1-1	Baxter	10,728
21		23	(a)	Leicester C	D	1-1	Bruce	10,481
22		26	(h)	Wrexham	W	2-1	Bruce, Jones (og)	17,820
23		30	(h)	Bristol R	D	1-1	Bruce	12,660
24	Feb	10	(h)	Brighton & HA	W	1-0	Bruce	11,649
25		24	(a)	Crystal Palace	D	0-0		17,592
26		28	(a)	Stoke C	D	1-1	Bruce	18,177
27	Mar	3	(h)	Fulham	D	2-2	Bruce, Potts	10,890
28		10	(a)	Burnley	D	1-1	Bruce	15,175
29		17	(h)	West Ham U	D	0-0		15,376
30		20	(h)	Oldham Ath	D	1-1	Coleman	12,535
31		24	(a)	Blackburn R	W	1-0	Bruce	17,790
32		31	(h)	Orient	D	1-1	Coleman	9,494
33	Apr	4	(a)	Newcastle U	L	3-4	Robinson 2, Bruce	12,157
34		7	(a)	Charlton Ath	D	1-1	Coleman	5,836
35		14	(a)	Wrexham	L	1-2	Robinson	13,419
36		16	(h)	Newcastle U	D	0-0		12,960
37		17	(h)	Leicester C	W	4-0	Robinson, Bruce 2, Coleman	10,394
38		21	(a)	Notts Co	D	0-0		7,009
39		24	(h)	Cambridge U	L	0-2		10,136
40		28	(h)	Luton T	D	2-2	Doyle, Coleman	8,927
41	May	5	(a)	Bristol R	W	1-0	Baxter	5,814
42		22	(a)	Millwall	W	2-0	Bell, Potts	2,833

FINAL LEAGUE POSITION: 7th in Division Two

Appearances

Sub. Appearances

Goals

Tunks	McMahon	Cameron	Doyle	Baxter	Cross	Burns	Haslegrave	Thomson	Robinson	Bruce	Wilson	Smith	Spavin	Potts	Coleman	Cochrane	Uzalac	O'Riordan	Taylor	Elliott	Bell	#
1	2	3	4	5	6	7	8	9	10	11												1
1		2*	4	5	6	7	8	9	10	11	3	12										2
1			4	5	6	7	2	9*	10	11	3		8	12								3
1			4	5	6	7	2	9	10	11	3		8*	12								4
1	2		6	5		4	8	10*	9	11	3	12		7								5
1	2		4	5		7	8	9	10*	11	3	12			6							6
1	2*		4	5		6	8			11	3	10		7	9	12						7
1		2*		5	6	4	8		9	11	3			10	7	12						8
1			4	5		10*	8	12		11	3			7	2	9	6					9
1	2	3	4	5			8	10	9	11				7				6				10
1	2	3	4	5			8	10	9	11				7				6*	12			11
1	2	3	4	5			8	10	9	11				7				6				12
1	2	3	4	5			8	10	9	11				7				6				13
1		3		5		4	8	10	9	11				7				6	2			14
1		3	12	5		4	8*	10	9	11				7				6	2			15
1		3	12	5		4	8	10*	9	11				7				6	2			16
1		3	4	5		10	8		9	11	12			7				6	2*			17
1		3		5		4	8		9	11				10	7			6	2			18
1		3		5		4	8*		9	11	12			10	7			6	2			19
1		3		5		4	8		9	11				10	7			6	2			20
1		3		5		4	8		9	11				10	7			6	2			21
1		3		5		4	8		9	11				10	7			6	2			22
1		3		5		4	8		9	11				10	7			6	2			23
1		3		5		4	8		9	11				10	7			6	2			24
1		3	12	5		4*	8		9	11				10	7			6	2			25
1		3	4	5			8		9	11				10	7			6	2			26
1		3	4	5			8		9	11				10	7			6	2			27
1		3	4	5			8		9	11				10	7			6	2			28
1		3	4*	5			8			11	12			10	7			6	2	9		29
1		3	4	5			8			11	12			10	7			6	2*	9		30
1		3	8	5						11				10	7			6	2	9	4	31
1		3	4*	5			8	12		11				10	9	7		6	2			32
1		3		5			8	12	9	11				10*	7			6	2		4	33
1		3		5			8		9	11				10	7			6	4	2		34
1		3		5			8		9	11*				10	7			6	2	12	4	35
1		3	12				8		9					10*	7		5	6	2	11	4	36
1		3	4				8		9	11					7		5	6	2	10		37
1		3	4				8		9*	11				12	7		5	6	2	10		38
1		3	4				8*		9	11				12	7		5	6	2	10		39
1		3	10				8		9	11					7		5	6	2	4		40
1		3	4	5			8		9	11				10	7			6	2*	12		41
1		3		5			8	12	9					10*	7		6		2	11	4	42
42	8	36	25	37	5	21	41	13	36	40	8	1	2	25	37	2	7	32	29	5	10	
			4					4			4	3		4		2			1	2		
			2	4		1		4	13	21				4	7	1					1	

1979-80

#	Month	Date		Opponent	Res	Score	Scorers	Att
1	Aug	18	(a)	Charlton Ath	W	3-0	Elliott, Bell, Thomson	6,148
2		21	(h)	Newcastle U	W	1-0	Potts	12,707
3		25	(h)	Swansea C	D	1-1	Bartley (og)	12,116
4	Sep	1	(a)	Fulham	L	0-1		7,922
5		8	(h)	West Ham U	D	1-1	Coleman	10,460
6		15	(a)	Oldham Ath	L	2-3	Thomson 2	9,849
7		22	(h)	Bristol R	W	3-2	Bruce 2, Elliott	7,555
8		29	(a)	Sunderland	D	1-1	Elliott	24,594
9	Oct	6	(h)	Birmingham C	D	0-0		10,740
10		10	(a)	Newcastle U	D	0-0		24,985
11		13	(a)	Q.P.R.	D	1-1	Thomson	14,316
12		20	(h)	Burnley	W	3-2	Bruce, Thomson 2	12,300
13		27	(a)	Luton T	D	1-1	Elliott	11,648
14	Nov	3	(h)	Charlton Ath	D	1-1	Elliott	9,950
15		10	(a)	Notts Co	L	1-2	Bruce	8,602
16		17	(h)	Leicester C	D	1-1	Bruce	10,038
17		24	(h)	Orient	D	2-2	Bruce, Elliott	7,835
18	Dec	1	(a)	Chelsea	L	0-2		21,192
19		8	(h)	Cambridge U	D	2-2	Bruce, Elliott	7,585
20		15	(a)	Cardiff C	W	2-0	Bruce 2	6,419
21		21	(h)	Watford	L	1-2	Elliott (pen)	8,956
22		26	(h)	Shrewsbury T	W	3-0	Elliott, Bruce, Bell	8,875
23		29	(a)	Swansea C	L	0-1		11,401
24	Jan	1	(a)	Wrexham	L	0-2		14,738
25		12	(h)	Fulham	W	3-2	Elliott 2 (1 pen), McGee	7,912
26		19	(a)	West Ham U	L	0-2		17,603
27	Feb	2	(h)	Oldham Ath	L	0-1		8,932
28		16	(h)	Sunderland	W	2-1	Hindmarch (og), Coleman	12,165
29		23	(h)	Q.P.R.	L	0-3		10,350
30	Mar	1	(a)	Burnley	D	1-1	McGee	10,843
31		8	(h)	Luton T	D	1-1	McGee	7,862
32		11	(a)	Bristol R	D	3-3	Baxter, McGee, Aitken (og)	6,022
33		15	(a)	Birmingham C	D	2-2	Elliott, McGee	19,548
34		22	(h)	Notts Co	W	2-0	McGee, Taylor	7,407
35		29	(a)	Leicester C	W	2-1	Elwiss 2	15,293
36	Apr	1	(a)	Shrewsbury T	W	3-1	Keay (og), Elliott 2	8,643
37		5	(h)	Wrexham	D	0-0		9,430
38		9	(a)	Watford	D	0-0		11,967
39		12	(h)	Chelsea	D	1-1	Baxter	13,069
40		19	(a)	Orient	D	2-2	McGee, Elliott	4,509
41		26	(h)	Cardiff C	W	2-0	McGee, Coleman	7,481
42	May	3	(a)	Cambridge U	L	2-3	Elliott, Elwiss	5,395

FINAL LEAGUE POSITION: 10th in Division Two

Appearances

Sub. Appearances

Goals

Tunks	Taylor	Wilson	Bell	Baxter	Blackley	Elliott	Haslegrave	Thomson	Doyle	Potts	Coleman	Cameron	O'Riordan	Bruce	Burns	McGee	McAteer	Naughton	Anderson	Houston	Elwiss	No.
1	2	3	4	5	6	7	8	9	10	11												1
1	2	3	7	5	6	9	8	11*	4	10	12											2
1	2	3	7	5	6	9		11	4	10	8											3
1		3	7	5	6*	9	8	11	4	10	12	2										4
1	2			5		9	8	11	4	10	7	3	6									5
1	2			5		9	8	11	4	10*	7	3	6	12								6
1	2	12		5	6	9	8			10	4*	3		11	7							7
1	2		7	5	6	9	8	12		10*		3		11	4							8
1	2		7	5	6	9	8			10		3		11	4							9
1	2		7	5	6	9	8			10		3		11	4							10
1	2		7	5	6	9	8			10		3		11	4							11
1	2		7	5	6	9*	8			10	12	3		11	4							12
1	2		7	5	6	9	8					3*		11	4	12						13
1	2	3	7	5	6	9	8			10				11	4							14
1	2	3	7	5	6	9	8			10				11	4							15
1	2	3*	7	5		9	8			12			6	11	4	10						16
1	2	3	7	5		9	8			10			6	11	4							17
1	2	3	7	5		9	8				12		6	11	4*	10						18
1	2	3	7	5		9	8				12		6	11	4	10*						19
1	2	3	7	5		9	8				10		6	11	4							20
1	2	3	7	5		9	8				10		6	11	4*	12						21
1	2		7	5		9				10	8		6	11	4		3					22
1	2		7	5		9	12			10*	8		6	11	4		3					23
1	2		7			9	8	4			11		6			10*	3	12				24
1	2		7			9	8	4					6	11		10	3		5			25
1	2		7			9	8	4			12		6	11		10*	3		5			26
1	2		7			9	8	4			12		6	11		10*	3		5			27
1	2		7		6	9		4			8		12	11			3	10*	5			28
1	2*		7		6	9		4			8			11			3	10	5	12		29
1			4	5	6	9	8			10	7	2		11			3					30
1	12		7	5	6	9	4*			10	8	2		11			3					31
1	2		7	5	6*	9				10	8			12	4	11	3					32
1	2		7	5		9				10*	8		6		4	11	3				12	33
1	2		7	5	6	9				10*	8				4	11	3				12	34
1	2		7*	5	6	9				12	8				4	11	3				10	35
1	2			5	6	9				7	8				4	11	3				10	36
1	2*			5	6	9				7	8		12		4	11	3				10	37
1				5	6	9				7	8	2			4	11	3				10	38
1				5	6	9				7	8	2	4			11	3				10	39
1			7	5	6*	9					8	2		12	4	11	3				10	40
1			7	5	6	9					8	2			4	11	3				10	41
1			7	5	6	9					8	2		12	4	11*	3				10	42
42	34	12	35	37	27	42	24	11	14	22	24	17	16	22	27	20	21	2	5		8	
	1		1				1	1			3	6		2	4	2	1			1	2	
		1	2	2		16		6			1	3		10		8					3	

29

1980-81

#	Month	Date		Opponent	Result	Score	Scorers	Attendance
1	Aug	16	(h)	Bristol C	D	1-1	Elliott	6,058
2		19	(a)	Grimsby T	D	0-0		10,461
3		23	(h)	West Ham U	D	0-0		9,063
4		30	(a)	Sheffield W	L	0-3		16,724
5	Sep	6	(h)	Cambridge U	W	2-0	McGee 2	5,516
6		13	(a)	Watford	L	1-2	Coleman	11,275
7		20	(a)	Chelsea	D	1-1	Elliott	13,755
8		27	(h)	Shrewsbury T	D	0-0		6,309
9	Oct	4	(a)	Orient	L	0-4		4,295
10		7	(h)	Newcastle U	L	2-3	Coleman, Bruce	5,301
11		11	(h)	Luton T	W	1-0	Elliott	5,620
12		18	(a)	Wrexham	W	1-0	Bruce	5,775
13		21	(a)	Bolton W	L	1-2	Bruce	10,713
14		25	(h)	Bristol C	D	0-0		5,807
15	Nov	1	(a)	Oldham Ath	D	1-1	Bruce	6,739
16		8	(h)	Cardiff C	W	3-1	Baxter, Bruce, Stevens (og)	5,458
17		15	(a)	Bristol C	D	0-0		8,042
18		22	(h)	Q.P.R.	W	3-2	Naughton 2, Baxter	6,725
19		28	(a)	Swansea C	L	0-3		9,115
20	Dec	2	(h)	Grimsby T	L	2-4	Elliott (pen), Baxter	5,289
21		6	(h)	Derby Co	L	0-3		6,118
22		13	(a)	Luton T	L	2-4	Elliott, Bruce	7,874
23		20	(h)	Wrexham	D	1-1	Elliott	4,746
24		26	(a)	Blackburn R	D	0-0		17,726
25		27	(h)	Notts Co	D	2-2	Baxter, Elliott (pen)	6,547
26	Jan	10	(a)	Q.P.R.	D	1-1	Bell	8,415
27		31	(a)	West Ham U	L	0-5		26,413
28	Feb	7	(h)	Watford U	W	2-1	McGee, Coleman	5,107
29		14	(a)	Cambridge U	L	0-1		4,228
30		21	(a)	Shrewsbury T	L	0-3		4,660
31		28	(h)	Chelsea	W	1-0	Bruce	8,129
32	Mar	7	(h)	Orient	W	3-0	Taylor (og), Doyle, McGee	5,448
33		14	(a)	Newcastle U	L	0-2		11,946
34		24	(h)	Bolton W	L	1-2	Bruce	8,505
35		28	(a)	Bristol R	L	0-2		4,427
36	Apr	4	(h)	Oldham Ath	L	1-2	Bruce	6,154
37		11	(a)	Cardiff C	W	3-1	Haslegrave, Bruce, Elliott	4,991
38		14	(h)	Sheffield W	W	2-1	Elliott, Houston	9,537
39		18	(a)	Notts Co	D	0-0		8,485
40		21	(h)	Blackburn R	D	0-0		18,742
41	May	2	(h)	Swansea C	L	1-3	Bruce	18,970
42		6	(a)	Derby Co	W	2-1	Bruce 2	15,050

FINAL LEAGUE POSITION: 20th in Division Two

Appearances

Sub. Appearances

Goals

Tunks	Taylor	Carmeron	Burns	Baxter	Blackley	Bell	Coleman	Elliott	Potts	McGee	Doyle	McAteer	Bruce	Sayer	O'Riordan	Houston	Westwell	Haslegrave	Naughton	Anderson	Litchfield	
1	2	3	4	5	6	7	8	9	10	11												1
1	2*	3	4	5	6	7	8	9	10	11	12											2
1		2	4	5	6*	7	8	9	10	11	12	3										3
1		2	4*	5	6	7	8			11	12	3	9	10								4
1		2	4	5		7	8			9		3	11		6	10						5
1		2	4	5		7	8	12		9		3	11	10*	6							6
1	3			5		7	8	10		9	4				6	11	2					7
1				5		7	8	12		9	4	3		10	6	11	2*					8
1	2			5	12		8	10		9	4	3		7	6	11*						9
1	2	3	4	5			8	9		12	7		10		6	11*						10
1		3	4	5	6		8	9		11	7		10		2							11
1		3	4	5	6		8	9		11	7		10		2							12
1			4	5	6	8		9		11	7	3	10		2							13
1	2		4	5	6		8	9		11	7*		10		3		12					14
1			4	5	6	7	8	9*		11		3	10		12		2					15
1	12		4	5		7	8			9		3	11		6		2	10*				16
1	12		4	5	6	7	8*	9		11		3	10				2					17
1	8		4	5	6	7		9		11		3					2		10			18
1	8	3	4	5	6	7		9		11			10				2		12			19
1	8	3	4	5	6*	7		9		11			10				2		12			20
1	4	3*		5		7		9		11	8		10	12			2			6		21
1	2		4	5		7		9		11*	8		10	12			3			6		22
1	2		4	5			8	9			7	3	10		6	11						23
1	2		4	5		7		9			8	3	10		6	11						24
1	2			5		4	7	9		12	8	3	10*		6	11						25
1				5		4	8	9		10	7	3			6	11	2					26
1				5		4	7	9		10*	8	3		12	6	11	2					27
1				5		4	8	9		10	7	3			6		2		11			28
1				5		4	8	9		10	7	3			6		2		11			29
1				5		4	8	9		10	7*	3	12		6		2		11			30
			3	5		4	8			10	7		12	9*			2		11	6	1	31
			3	5		4	8			10	7		9				2		11	6	1	32
			3	5		4	8	12		10	7		9*				2		11	6*	1	33
1			3	5	12	4	8			10	7		9				2		11	6*		34
1				5	6	12	8	9		11	7	3	10				2*	4				35
1	2	3		5	6	8	9			11	7					10		4				36
1	2		3	5	6	8	7	9					11			10		4				37
1	2		3	5	6	8	7	9					11			10		4				38
1	2		3	5	6	8	7	9					11			10		4				39
1	2		3	5	6	8	7	9					11			10		4				40
1	2		3*	5	6	8	7	9					11			10		4		12		41
1	2			5	6	8	7	9					11		12	10*		4	3			42
39	20	13	29	42	21	34	36	32	3	32	24	20	29	5	19	17	20	8	9	7	3	
	2			2	1		3			2	3		2	3	2			1	1	1		
			4		1	3	9			4	1		13			1		1	2			

1981-82

1	Aug	29	(a)	Millwall	L	1-2	Walsh	4,549
2	Sep	5	(h)	Portsmouth	W	1-0	Bruce	6,112
3		12	(a)	Swindon T	L	0-4		5,695
4		19	(h)	Gillingham	D	1-1	Bruce (pen)	4,563
5		22	(h)	Huddersfield T	D	1-1	Naughton	6,483
6		26	(a)	Newport Co	D	1-1	Doyle	5,064
7		29	(a)	Doncaster R	L	0-1		7,513
8	Oct	3	(h)	Bristol R	L	0-1		4,964
9		10	(a)	Bristol C	D	0-0		5,389
10		17	(h)	Reading	D	0-0		5,671
11		20	(h)	Burnley	D	1-1	O'Riordan	7,527
12		24	(a)	Exeter C	L	3-4	Bruce 2 (1 pen), Doyle	3,642
13		31	(h)	Southend U	W	1-0	Pountney (og)	4,285
14	Nov	4	(a)	Lincoln C	W	2-1	Buckley, Elliott	3,587
15		7	(h)	Chester	L	0-1		5,181
16		14	(a)	Wimbledon	L	2-3	Dunn, Bruce	2,428
17		28	(a)	Oxford U	L	0-3		3,798
18	Dec	5	(h)	Brentford	L	1-3	Bruce	4,162
19	Jan	5	(a)	Chesterfield	D	0-0		3,964
20		16	(h)	Plymouth Argyle	W	1-0	Bruce	4,936
21		23	(h)	Millwall	W	1-0	Elliott (pen)	5,085
22		30	(a)	Gillingham	W	2-0	Naughton, Bruce	5,379
23	Feb	2	(a)	Carlisle U	L	0-1		5,044
24		6	(h)	Swindon T	D	0-0		5,606
25		9	(a)	Huddersfield T	W	3-2	Bruce 2, Elliott	6,674
26		13	(a)	Bristol R	L	0-2		5,003
27		20	(h)	Doncaster R	W	3-1	McGee, Bruce, Elliott (pen)	5,830
28		27	(h)	Bristol C	L	1-3	Kelly	6,411
29	Mar	6	(a)	Reading	L	1-2	Elliott	2,655
30		13	(h)	Exeter C	W	1-0	Elliott	4,770
31		16	(h)	Lincoln C	D	1-1	O'Riordan	4,879
32		19	(a)	Southend U	D	2-2	Elliott, Bruce	3,549
33		27	(a)	Chester	W	1-0	Elliott	2,842
34	Apr	3	(h)	Wimbledon	W	3-2	Bruce 2, O'Riordan	4,964
35		6	(a)	Portsmouth	D	1-1	O'Riordan	6,712
36		10	(h)	Carlisle U	D	0-1		7,802
37		13	(a)	Walsall	W	3-0	Elliott, Bruce 2	3,507
38		17	(a)	Brentford	D	0-0		5,627
39		20	(h)	Fulham	L	1-3	Buckley (pen)	6,009
40		24	(h)	Oxford U	D	2-2	Kelly, Doyle	5,516
41		27	(h)	Walsall	W	1-0	Kelly	4,930
42	May	1	(a)	Plymouth Argyle	W	3-0	Kelly, Bell, Elliott	3,319
43		4	(h)	Newport Co	W	2-1	Bruce, Kelly	4,972
44		8	(h)	Chesterfield	W	2-0	Naughton, Bruce	5,445
45		11	(a)	Burnley	L	0-2		13,871
46		15	(a)	Fulham	L	0-3		7,985

FINAL LEAGUE POSITION: 14th in Division Three

Appearances

Sub. Appearances

Goals

Litchfield	Taylor	Coleman	Clark	O'Riordan	Blackley	Walsh	Houston	Bruce	Doyle	Naughton	Elliott	Westwell	McGee	McAteer	Anderson	Bell	Farrelly	Booth	Kelly	Buckley	Dunn	Mullen	Sayer	Hodge	
1	2	3	4	5	6	7	8	9	10	11*	12														1
1		2	4	5	6	12	7*	10	8	11		3	9												2
1	2		4	5	6	12	7	10	8*	11		3	9												3
1	2		4	5		12	7	9		11	10*			3	6	8									4
1	2		4	5		7	8	9		11*				3	6	10	12								5
1	2		4	5		11	7	9	8					3	6	10									6
1	2	6		5		7*	12	9	8			11		3	4	10									7
1	2		4	5		12	7	9	8*			11		3	6	10									8
1	2		4	6				9						3	10*	12		5	7	8	11				9
1	2		4	6				9						3	10*	12		5	7	8	11				10
1	12	2	4	6				9	10					3				5	7	8	11*				11
1	8		4	6				9	10		2			3	12			5*	7		11				12
1	2		4	6				9	10					3	5	12			7*	8	11				13
1	2		4	6				9	10		8			3	12			5*	7		11				14
1	2*		4	6				9	10		8			3	5	12			7		11				15
1	2*		4	6				9	10	12	8			3	5				7		11				16
1	12	2		4			7	8*	10	11	9			3				5				6			17
1	2	8	4					9	6		10			3	7			5					11		18
	2			6				11	8	10	9			3	7*	4		5		12				1	19
	2			6				11	8	10	9			3	7	4		5						1	20
	2			6				11	8	10	9			3	7	4		5						1	21
	2			6				11	8	10	9			3	7*	4		5		12				1	22
				6		12		11	8	10	9	2		3	4*			5	7					1	23
				6		12		11	8	10	9	2*		3	4			5	7					1	24
	2			6				11	8	10	9			3	4			5	7					1	25
				6				11		10*	9		8	3	2	4		5	7	12				1	26
	2			6				11		10	9		8	3	5	4			7					1	27
	2*			6				11		10	9		8	3	12	4		5	7					1	28
				6				11		12	9		8	3	2	4		5*	7	10				1	29
				6				11			9		8	3	2	4		5	7	10				1	30
				6				11			9		8	3	2	4		5	7	10				1	31
				6		12		11	8		9			3	2	4*		5	7	10				1	32
				6				11	8	4	9			3	2			5	7	10				1	33
				6				11	8	4	9			3	2			5	7	10				1	34
				6				11	8	4	9			3	2*			5	7	10				1	35
				6		12		11	8	4	9			3	2			5	7	10*				1	36
				6				11	8	4	9			3	2			5	7	10				1	37
				6				11	8	4	9			3	2			5	7	10				1	38
				6		12		11	8	4	9			3	2			5*	7	10				1	39
				6		12		11	8	4	9	5		3	2				7	10*				1	40
				6		12		11	8	4	9*	5		3	2	10			7					1	41
				6				11	8	4	9	5		3	2	10			7					1	42
				6			4	11	8	3	9	5			2	10			7					1	43
				6				11	8	4	9	5		3	2	10			7					1	44
				6		12		11	8	4	9	5		3	2	10*			7					1	45
				6		12		11	8	4	9	5		3	2	10			7*					1	46
18	10	15	18	46	3	4	9	46	36	31	34	12	10	41	35	22	3	27	28	20	8	1	1	28	
	2					6	9		2	1			3		4				2	2					
			4	1				18	3	3	10		1		1				5	2					

1982-83

1	Aug	28	(h)	Millwall	W	3-2	Elliott 3 (1 pen)	4,483
2	Sep	4	(a)	Sheffield U	L	1-2	Kelly	14,527
3		7	(a)	Walsall	L	1-2	McAteer	2,060
4		11	(h)	Oxford U	L	1-2	Elliott	4,481
5		18	(a)	Exeter C	L	1-5	Elliott (pen)	2,310
6		25	(h)	Bristol R	D	2-2	Bell, Elliott	3,880
7		28	(h)	Wrexham	W	3-0	O'Riordan, Elliott 2	3,363
8	Oct	2	(a)	Reading	W	3-2	Elliott 2, Bruce	1,713
9		9	(a)	Gillingham	L	1-2	Bruce	4,390
10		16	(h)	Huddersfield T	D	0-0		5,570
11		19	(h)	Newport Co	D	0-0		3,747
12		23	(a)	Portsmouth	L	1-3	Bruce	10,331
13		30	(h)	Bournemouth	L	0-1		3,589
14	Nov	2	(a)	Brentford	L	1-3	Elliott	6,142
15		6	(a)	Cardiff C	L	1-3	O'Riordan	5,546
16		13	(h)	Chesterfield	D	1-1	Houston	3,574
17		27	(h)	Plymouth Argyle	D	2-2	McAteer, Elliott	3,633
18	Dec	3	(a)	Southend U	W	3-2	Elliott, Houston, Walsh	3,749
19		17	(a)	Orient	L	1-2	Coleman	1,668
20		27	(h)	Bradford C	D	0-0		7,238
21		28	(a)	Doncaster R	L	0-2		3,895
22	Jan	1	(h)	Wigan Ath	W	4-1	Bruce 2, McAteer, Kelly (pen)	7,565
23		3	(a)	Lincoln C	L	0-3		5,891
24		15	(a)	Millwall	L	0-1		2,816
25		22	(h)	Exeter C	D	2-2	Elliott, Bruce	3,767
26		29	(a)	Oxford U	L	2-3	Gowling, Naughton	4,441
27	Feb	5	(a)	Wrexham	L	1-3	Bell	1,920
28		15	(a)	Newport Co	L	0-3		2,317
29		19	(h)	Gillingham	D	0-0		3,479
30		26	(a)	Huddersfield T	D	1-1	O'Riordan	8,562
31	Mar	1	(h)	Brentford	W	3-0	Elliott, Bell, Westwell	3,669
32		5	(h)	Portsmouth	D	0-0		5,610
33		12	(a)	Bournemouth	L	0-4		4,407
34		19	(h)	Cardiff C	W	2-1	Bruce, Elliott	4,608
35		26	(a)	Chesterfield	D	1-1	O'Riordan	2,332
36		29	(h)	Walsall	W	1-0	Sayer	4,013
37	Apr	2	(h)	Doncaster R	W	4-1	Hinnigan, McAteer, Elliott, Humphries (og)	5,287
38		4	(a)	Bradford C	W	2-1	Gowling, McAteer (pen)	4,357
39		8	(h)	Southend U	D	1-1	Bell	6,286
40		12	(h)	Sheffield U	W	1-0	Houston S (og)	6,296
41		16	(a)	Bristol R	L	2-3	Elliott, Hinnigan	5,189
42		23	(h)	Orient	W	2-1	Hinnigan, Sayer	5,628
43		30	(a)	Plymouth Argyle	D	1-1	Booth	2,912
44	May	2	(h)	Lincoln C	W	1-0	Gowling	6,537
45		7	(h)	Reading	W	2-0	Gowling, Elliott	7,253
46		14	(a)	Wigan Ath	W	1-0	Gowling	7,191

FINAL LEAGUE POSITION: 16th in Division Three

Appearances

Sub. Appearances

Goals

Litchfield	Walsh	McAteer	O'Riordan	Westwell	Coleman	Kelly	Bell	Elliott	Naughton	Bruce	Houston	Gowling	Buckley	Arnold (L)	Clark	Campbell	Sayer	Booth	Farrelly	Lodge	Hunter	Hodge(L)	Hinnigan	
1	2	3	4	5	6	7*	8	9	10	11	12													1
1	2	3	4	5		7	8	9	10	11*	12	6												2
1	2	3	4	5		7	8	9	10	11		6												3
1	2	3	4	5		7	8	9	10	12	11*	6												4
1	2	3	4	5*	12	7	8	9	10		11	6												5
1	2	3	4	5	12	7	8	9	10*		11	6												6
1	2	3	4	5		7	8	9	10		11	6												7
1	2	3		5	4	7	8	9	10	12	11*	6												8
1	2*	3		5	4	7	8	9	10	11		6	12											9
	2	3		5	4*	7	8	9	10	11		6	12	1										10
	2*	3		5		7	8	9	10	11		6	12	1	4									11
	2*	3		5		7	8	9	10	11		6	12	1	4									12
	2*	3	12	5		7	8	9	10	11		6		1	4									13
	5	3*	4	2		7	8	9		11	12	6	10	1										14
		4	2	5		7	8	9	3*	11	12	6	10	1										15
		3	4	2	5	7		9	12		11	6	10*			1	8							16
1	7	3	4	2	5			9	10		11	6					8							17
1	7	3	4	2	5			9	10		11	6					8							18
1	7	3	4	2	5			9	10*		11	6	12				8							19
1	7	3	4	2	5*		12	9	10		11	6					8							20
1	7	3	4	2		10	5	9		12	11	6					8*							21
1	7	3	4	5		2		9	10		11	6					8							22
1	7	3	4	5		2		9	10		11	6					8							23
1		3	2			7	9		10	8	11	6	4					5						24
1		3	4	2		7	11	9	10	8		6						5						25
1		3	4	2		7*	11	9	10	12	8	6						5						26
1		3	4	2		7*	11	9	10	8		6	5						12					27
1	7	3	4	5			11	9	10	8*									2	6	12			28
1	7*	3	4	5	12		11	9	10	8									2	6				29
1	7	3	4	5	12		11	9	10	8									2*	6				30
	7	3	4	5	2*		11	9	10	8	12									6		1		31
	7*	3	4	5	2		11	9	10	8	12									6		1		32
	7*	3	4	5	2	12	11	9	10	8										6		1		33
		3	4	5*			11	9	10	8							7			6		1	2	34
		3	4			12	11	9	10	8							7*	5		6		1	2	35
		3	4				11	9	10	8							7	5		6		1	2	36
		3	4				11	9	10	8							7	5		6		1	2	37
		3	4				11	9	10	8							7*	5		6		1	2	38
		3	4				11	9	10	8	12						7	5		6		1	2	39
			4				11	9	10	8							7	5	2	6		1	3	40
		3*	4			12	11	9	10	8							7	5		6		1	2	41
		3	4				11	9	10		12	8*					7	5		6		1	2	42
		3	4			12	11	9	10			8*					7	5		6		1	2	43
		3	4				11	9	10	8							7	5		6		1	2	44
		3	4				11	9	10	8							7	5		6		1	2	45
	5	3				12	8	10	11			9*					7	4		6		1	2	46
23	27	44	40	31	15	23	39	45	40	22	15	37	7	6	3	1	21	15	4	19	0	16	13	
			1		3	6	1		1	5	5	3	5						1		1			
	1	5	4	1	1	2	4	19	1	7	2	5					2	1					3	

1983-84

1	Aug	27	(a)	Bournemouth	W	1-0	Houston		4,163
2	Sep	3	(h)	Brentford	D	3-3	Kelly 2, Sayer		3,799
3		6	(h)	Southend U	W	4-1	Sayer, Kelly, Elliott 2		3,967
4		10	(a)	Sheffield U	D	1-1	Sayer		12,441
5		17	(h)	Hull C	D	0-0			6,661
6		24	(a)	Plymouth Argyle	L	0-1			3,674
7		27	(a)	Newport Co	D	1-1	Elliott (pen)		2,542
8	Oct	1	(h)	Oxford U	L	1-2	Sayer		4,665
9		8	(a)	Gillingham	L	0-2			3,725
10		15	(h)	Wigan Ath	L	2-3	Elliott (pen), Hinnigan		6,622
11		18	(h)	Wimbledon	L	2-3	Elliott 2		3,515
12		21	(a)	Millwall	L	0-1			5,243
13		29	(h)	Lincoln C	L	1-2	Clark		4,458
14	Nov	1	(a)	Bristol R	L	1-3	Farrelly		5,635
15		5	(a)	Burnley	L	1-2	Houghton		7,915
16		12	(h)	Rotherham U	W	1-0	Hinnigan		3,196
17		26	(h)	Exeter C	W	2-1	Kelly 2		3,373
18	Dec	3	(a)	Orient	L	1-2	D Jones		2,679
19		17	(a)	Bolton W	D	2-2	Houghton, Farnworth (og)		6,275
20		26	(h)	Port Vale	W	4-0	Houghton 2, Elliott, Kelly		5,599
21		27	(a)	Scunthorpe U	W	5-1	Elliott 3, Houghton, Kelly		3,986
22		31	(h)	Walsall	L	0-1			6,226
23	Jan	2	(a)	Bradford C	L	2-3	Naughton, Kelly		6,405
24		14	(h)	Bournemouth	W	2-0	Houghton, Clark (pen)		3,476
25		31	(h)	Sheffield U	D	2-2	Farrelly, Walsh		5,023
26	Feb	4	(a)	Oxford U	L	0-2			9,105
27		11	(h)	Plymouth Argyle	W	2-1	Twentyman, Naughton		4,370
28		14	(a)	Bristol R	W	1-0	Clark		3,813
29		18	(a)	Lincoln C	L	1-2	Naughton		2,780
30		25	(h)	Millwall	D	0-0			4,109
31	Mar	3	(a)	Wimbledon	D	2-2	Booth, Hinnigan		2,524
32		6	(h)	Burnley	W	4-2	Elliott, Kelly, Hinnigan, Houghton		8,745
33		10	(a)	Rotherham U	W	1-0	Hinnigan		3,256
34		17	(h)	Gillingham	D	2-2	Twentyman, Elliott		3,874
35		24	(a)	Wigan Ath	L	0-1			4,470
36		30	(h)	Newport Co	W	2-0	Elliott, Kelly		3,534
37	Apr	3	(a)	Brentford	L	1-4	Houston		3,446
38		6	(a)	Southend U	D	1-1	Kelly		1,826
39		10	(a)	Hull C	L	0-3			8,134
40		14	(h)	Orient	W	3-1	Houghton, Kelly, Houston		3,144
41		21	(a)	Port Vale	D	1-1	Houghton		3,574
42		24	(h)	Scunthorpe U	W	1-0	Elliott		3,403
43		28	(a)	Exeter C	L	1-2	Elliott		2,005
44	May	5	(h)	Bradford C	L	1-2	Clark (pen)		3,242
45		7	(a)	Walsall	L	1-2	Kelly		3,273
46		12	(h)	Bolton W	W	2-1	Clark, Elliott		5,077

FINAL LEAGUE POSITION: 16th in Division Three

Appearances

Sub. Appearances

Goals

Litchfield	Hinnigan	McAteer	Jones D	Booth	Lodge	Kelly	Sayer	Elliott	Naughton	Houston	Telfer	Bleasdale	Clark	Walsh	Farrelly	Twentyman	Houghton	Jones M	Murphy	Cameron	#
1	2	3	4	5	6	7	8	9	10	11											1
1	2	3*	4	5	6	7	8	9		11	12	10									2
1	2	3	4	5	6	7	8	9		11*	12	10									3
1		3	4	5	6	7	8	9	12	11*		10	2								4
1		3	4	5	6	7	8	9	12	11		10*	2								5
1	12	3	4*	5	6		8	9	10	11			2	7							6
1	3		4	5	6		8	9	10	11				7	2						7
1	2	3	4	5*	6		8		10	11	12			7		9					8
1	2	3	4		6		8	9	10*	12			7			5	11				9
1	2	3	4		6		8	9	10	12			7*			5	11				10
1		3		5	6			9	12	7			10	8*	2	4	11				11
1		3	4	5	6			9		7			10	8	2*	12	11				12
1		3	4	5	6			9	12	7			10	8	2		11*				13
1		3	4	5	6			9	11	7			10*	8	2	12					14
1		3	4	5	6	7		9	8				10		2		11				15
1	2	3	4	5	6	7		9	8*				10			12	11				16
1	2	3	4		6	7		9	8	12			10			5*	11				17
1	2	3	4	5		7		9	8*	12			10		6		11				18
1	2	3	4	5		7		9	10	12				8	6*		11				19
1	2	3	4	5		7		9	10					8	6		11				20
1	2	3*	4	5		7		9	10	12				8	6		11				21
1	3		4	5		7		9	10	12			2	8	6*		11				22
1	3		4	5		7		9	10				2	8	6		11				23
1	3		4	5*		7		9	10	12			2	8	6		11				24
1	3		4			7*		9	10	12			2	8	6	5	11				25
1	3		4			7		9	10	12			2	8*	6	5	11				26
1	3	12	4			7		9	10				2	8	6	5	11*				27
1	3	12	4			7		9	10	11			2	8*	6	5					28
1	2	3	4	12				9	10	11			6	8	7*	5					29
1	2	3	4					9	10	12			6	8*	7	5	11				30
1	2	3	4				8	9	10	12			6		7	5	11				31
1	2	3	4			7		9	10	12			6	8		5	11*				32
1	2	3	4			7		9	10	12			6	8*		5	11				33
1	2	3	4			7		9	10	12			6*	8		5	11				34
1	2	3	4	5		7		9	10	12			6	8			11*				35
1	2	3	4	5		7	11	9	10	12			6*	8							36
1	2	3				7	6*	9	10	11				8		5	12				37
1	2	3		5		7	6*	9	10	11				8		4	12				38
1	2	3	4	12		7		9	10	11			6*		5	8					39
1		3	4	5		7			10	12			6			9*	11	2	8		40
1	2	3	4*	5		7		9	12	11			6				10		8		41
	3*			5		7		9	12	11			6		2	4	10		8	1	42
1	3			5		7		9	12	11			6		2	4	10		8*		43
1	4					7	8	9		11			6		2	5	10	3			44
1	3					7	8*	9	10	11			6			4	5	2	12		45
1	3			5				9	10	11			6		7	4	8	2			46
45	38	32	37	31	17	34	15	44	35	23		4	31	25	31	25	30	4	4	1	
	1	2		2					7	18	2	1			3	2			1		
	5		1	1		13	4	16	3	3			5		2	2	10				

1984-85

1	Aug	25	(h)	Doncaster R	W	2-0	Houston, Wilkins	3,741
2	Sep	1	(a)	Bristol R	L	0-3		5,357
3		8	(h)	Derby Co	W	2-1	Houghton, Kelly	5,425
4		15	(a)	Hull C	W	2-1	Clark, D Jones	7,323
5		18	(a)	Cambridge U	W	3-0	Houston, Houghton, Wilkins	2,310
6		22	(h)	Rotherham U	L	0-3		3,063
7		29	(a)	Plymouth Argyle	L	4-6	Clarke 2, Kelly 2 (1 pen)	4,258
8	Oct	2	(h)	Orient	L	0-1		3,683
9		6	(a)	Lincoln C	L	0-4		1,906
10		13	(h)	Reading	L	0-2		3,656
11		20	(a)	Bolton W	L	0-4		5,691
12		23	(h)	Bradford C	L	1-4	Greenwood	3,588
13		27	(a)	Bournemouth	L	0-2		3,509
14	Nov	3	(h)	Burnley	D	3-3	Greenwood 2, Kelly	5,003
15		6	(h)	Swansea C	W	3-2	Clark, Greenwood, Houston	3,200
16		10	(a)	Millwall	L	0-3		5,680
17		24	(h)	Bristol	W	3-2	Houston, Jones, M Naughton	3,902
18	Dec	1	(a)	Gillingham	L	0-4		455
19		15	(h)	Brentford	D	1-1	Gibson	2,808
20		19	(h)	York C	L	2-4	Johnson (pen), Rudge	2,864
21		26	(a)	Walsall	L	1-2	Greenwood	5,856
22		29	(a)	Wigan Ath	L	0-2		4,503
23	Jan	1	(h)	Newport Co	D	1-1	Kelly	3,375
24		12	(a)	Bristol R	D	2-2	Johnson, Twentyman	3,136
25	Feb	2	(h)	Plymouth Argyle	L	1-2	Kelly	3,248
26		9	(a)	Rotherham U	L	0-3		3,645
27		23	(a)	Burnley	L	0-0		4,740
28		26	(h)	Cambridge U	W	3-1	Brazil, Clark, Farrelly	2,653
29	Mar	2	(h)	Bournemouth	W	2-1	Farrelly, Johnson	2,991
30		6	(a)	Bradford C	L	0-3		6,345
31		9	(h)	Bolton W	W	1-0	Gibson	5,478
32		13	(a)	Derby Co	L	0-2		8,248
33		16	(a)	Reading	L	0-3		3,053
34		23	(h)	Lincoln C	L	0-1		2,926
35		26	(a)	Doncaster R	W	2-1	Kelly, Rudge	2,684
36		30	(a)	Swansea C	L	1-4	Brazil	2,380
37	Apr	6	(h)	Walsall	W	1-0	Houghton	3,776
38		8	(a)	Newport Co	D	3-3	Houghton, McAteer, Twentyman	2,199
39		13	(h)	Millwall	W	2-1	Brazil, Houston	3,855
40		20	(a)	Bristol C	L	0-4		9,637
41		23	(h)	Hull C	L	1-4	Gibson	4,636
42		27	(h)	Gillingham	D	0-0		3,190
43		30	(a)	Orient	D	0-0		3,162
44	May	4	(a)	Brentford	L	1-3	Houghton	3,476
45		6	(h)	Wigan Ath	L	2-5	Houghton, McAteer (pen)	4,875
46		11	(a)	York C	W	1-0	Stevens	4,523

FINAL LEAGUE POSITION: 23rd in Division Three

Appearances

Sub. Appearances

Goals

Litchfield	Jones M	McAteer	Twentyman	Booth	Clark	Kelly	Rudge	Naughton	Houston	Houghton	Jones D	Farrelly	Murphy	Johnson	Gray	Welsh	Campbell	Gidson	Wealands	Atkins	Brazil	Platt	Stevens	Greenwood	Wilkins	#
1	2	3	4	5	6	7	8	10*	11	12														9		1
1		3	4	5	12	7	8		10	11	2*	6												9		2
1	2		4	5	6	7	3		10	11	9	8														3
1	2		4	5	6		3		10	11	9	8	7													4
1	2*		4	5	6		3		10	11	9	8	7											12		5
1	2		4	5	6		3		10	11	9	8	7*											12		6
1	2		4	5	6	7	3		10	11	9	8														7
1	3		4	5	6	7	8		10	11	9	2*												12		8
1	2		4	5*		7	3		11	10		6	8											12	9	9
1	2		5			7	3		10	11*	4	6		9										8		10
1	2	3	5			7			10	11	8	4	6	9												11
1	2	3	5		6	7			10	12	4	8		9*										11		12
1	2	3	5		6	7			10	11	12	4												8		13
1	2	3	5		6	7			10	11		4		8										9		14
1	2	3*	5	4	6	7			10	11				8										9		15
1	2	3	5	4	6	7			10	11				8										9		16
1	2	3			6				10	11	4			9	8	5										17
1	2	3			6				10	11	4				8	5										18
		3	4		6	7		10				2		9	8		1	5						12		19
		3	4		6	7	12	10*				2		9	8		1	5						11		20
		3	4		6	7	11	12				2		10	9			5*	1					8		21
		3	5		6	7	8	10				2		9*	4				1					11		22
		3	5		6	7	8	10		9		2			4				1					11		23
		3	4		6	7	8*	10		11		2		12				5	1							24
		3	4		6	7	8	10*	12	11		2		9			1	5								25
		3	5		6	7		10	11*			2		8	4		1	9						12		26
	2	3	9		6	8	12	10	7								1	5*		4	11					27
	2	3	5		6	12	8	9	7					10*						4	11	1				28
	2*	3	5		6	12	8	9	7					10						4	11	1				29
		3	5			7	8	9				2		10				6		4	11	1				30
	2	3	5			7	8	9	12			4		10*				6			11	1				31
	2	3	5		6		8	9	10			7		4							11	1				32
	2	3	5		6	7	8	9		11				10*						4		1	12			33
	2	3	5		6	7		9	8	11				10*						4		1	12			34
		3	5		6	7	8*		11	9		2		12			1			4	10					35
		3	5		6	7			9*			2		12			1	8		4	11		10			36
	2	3	9		6	7				11				8			1	5		4	10					37
	2	3	9		6	7				11				8			1	5		4	10					38
		3	9		6	7				11		2		8			1	5		4	10					39
		3	9		6	7				11		2	12	8*			1	5		4	10					40
	2	3	9		6	7			12			11*		8			1	5		4	10					41
	2	3	5		6	7		9*	10			4		8			1				11			12		42
	2	3	5		6	7		9				4		8	10		1				11					43
		3	5		6	7		9				4		8	10		1			2	11					44
	2	3	5		6	7		9				4		8			1			10	11					45
	2		5			7		9	3	6		10*		12			1			4	11		8			46
18	35	33	44	11	38	34	23	31	26	22	13	39	5	20	13	2	17	17	4	13	17	7	3	11	3	
			1	2	1	2		5	2					4	1								1	4	3	
	2	2	2	5	7	2	1	5	6	2				3				3			3		1	5	2	

39

1985-86

1	Aug	17	(h)	Peterborough U	L	2-4	Brazil, Thomas	3,177
2		26	(h)	Tranmere R	D	2-2	Brazil (pen), Thomas	4,206
3		30	(a)	Halifax T	L	1-2	Greenwood	2,011
4	Sep	7	(h)	Torquay U	W	4-0	Brazil 2, Greenwood 2	3,403
5		10	(a)	Northampton T	L	0-6		2,171
6		13	(h)	Stockport Co	L	1-2	Thomas	3,436
7		17	(h)	Burnley	W	1-0	Thomas	5,585
8		28	(h)	Hereford U	W	2-0	Greenwood, Brazil	3,397
9	Oct	2	(a)	Cambridge U	L	0-2		1,500
10		5	(a)	Crewe Alex	D	3-3	Brazil, Gibson, Greenwood	2,454
11		12	(h)	Chester C	L	3-6	Foster, Welsh, Brazil (pen)	4,073
12		19	(a)	Rochdale	D	1-1	Brazil	2,527
13		22	(h)	Hartlepool U	W	2-1	Greenwood, Foster	3,538
14		25	(a)	Southend U	L	1-2	Greenwood	2,787
15	Nov	2	(h)	Port Vale	L	0-1		4,531
16		5	(h)	Scunthorpe U	L	0-1		2,007
17		9	(a)	Orient	L	0-2		2,805
18		23	(h)	Colchester U	W	3-2	Thomas, Gray, Stevens	2,793
19		30	(a)	Exeter C	L	3-0		1,896
20	Dec	7	(a)	Swindon T	L	1-4	Allatt (pen)	3,945
21		14	(h)	Aldershot	L	1-3	Thomas	2,746
22		21	(h)	Northampton T	D	1-1	Thomas	2,570
23		26	(a)	Wrexham	D	1-1	Atkins	2,217
24	Jan	1	(h)	Mansfield T	L	0-2		3,705
25		4	(a)	Port Vale	W	1-0	Jones	3,592
26		11	(h)	Halifax T	L	0-1		3,184
27		18	(a)	Peterborough U	D	1-1	Allatt	2,711
28		24	(a)	Stockport Co	L	1-2	Thomas	3,035
29	Feb	1	(a)	Torquay U	L	0-1		1,215
30		5	(a)	Hartlepool U	L	0-1		3,102
31		8	(h)	Rochdale	D	1-1	Greenwood	3,266
32		22	(h)	Swindon T	L	0-3		3,361
33	Mar	1	(a)	Hereford U	D	1-1	Brazil	1,857
34		8	(h)	Crewe Alex	L	1-2	Thomas	2,922
35		15	(a)	Chester C	L	0-2		3,062
36		18	(h)	Cambridge U	L	1-2	Brazil (pen)	2,840
37		22	(h)	Southend U	W	3-2	Brazil (pen), Thomas 2	2,623
38		25	(a)	Tranmere R	W	3-2	Brazil, Thomas 2	1,574
39		29	(a)	Mansfield T	W	3-2	Foster, Atkins, Allatt	3,733
40		31	(h)	Wrexham	W	1-0	Thomas	5,163
41	Apr	4	(a)	Scunthorpe U	W	3-1	Thomas 2, Greenwood	2,261
42		12	(h)	Orient	L	1-3	Brazil (pen)	4,750
43		18	(a)	Colchester U	L	0-4		2,046
44		22	(a)	Burnley	D	1-1	Brazil (pen)	3,787
45		26	(h)	Exeter C	D	2-2	Thomas, Gibson	3,132
46	May	3	(a)	Aldershot	L	0-4		1,866

FINAL LEAGUE POSITION: 23rd in Division Four

Appearances

Sub. Appearances

Goals

Platt	Jones	McAteer	Atkins	Twentyman	Gray	Keen	Foster	Thomas	Rudge	Brazil	Greenwood	Clark	Welsh	Gibson	Martin	Chippendale	Stevens	Rodgers	Tottoh	Allatt	McNeil	Reid	Cooper	Harrington	Kelly	Pilling	Jemson	
1	2	3	4	5	6*	7	8	9	10	11	12																	1
1	2	3	4	5		7	8	9	10	11		6																2
1	2	3*	4	5		7	8	9	10	11	12	6																3
1	2	3	4	5		7	8	9*	10	11	12	6																4
1	2	3	4*	5		7	8		10	11	9	6	12															5
1	2		4	3		7		9	10	11	8	6		5														6
1	3		4	2		7	8	9		11	10	6*	12	5														7
1	3		4	2	10	7		9		11	8			5	6													8
1	3		4	2	10	7		9		11*	8		12	5	6													9
1	3		4	2	10	7		9		11	8			5	6													10
1	3		4	2	7*		8	9		11			12	5	6	10												11
1			2	10*		7	8		3	11	9		4	5	6	12												12
1	3			2		7	8		10	11	9		4	5	6													13
1	3		5		2		8		10	11	9		4		6	7												14
1	3	8	2						10	11	9		4	5	6	7*	12											15
1	3	4	2						10*	11	9			5		7	6	8	12									16
1	3	4	2					12	10	11	9*			5		7	6			8								17
1	3	4	5	8				9	2	11					6		7			10								18
1	3		5	8			12	9	2	11*			4		6		7			10								19
1	3		5	8*			4	9	2	11			12		6		7			10								20
1	8*	3	5					9		11	12				6		7			10	2	4						21
1	8		4	5				9	3	7					6					10	2		11					22
1	3		4	5				9	8	11					6					10	2	7*	12					23
1	3		4	5				9		11					6					10	2	7	8					24
1	3	7	4	5	8			9		11					6					10	2							25
1	3*	7	4	5	8			9		11					6					10	2		12					26
1	3	7	4		5	12		9		11					6*					10	2		8					27
1	8	3	4			7	12	9		11				5	6					10*	2							28
1	8	3	4			7	12	9		11				5	6					10*	2							29
1	8		4		7	2	10	9*		11	12			5	6						3							30
1	4	3			8	7	10	12		11*	9			5	6						2							31
	4	3			8	7	10	12		11	9			5	6*						2			1				32
	4	3			8	7	10	12		11	9		6	5							2			1*				33
	4	3	6		8	7*	10	12		11	9			5							2				1			34
	4	3			8	7	10	5		11	9				6						2				1			35
	4	3			8	7*	10	12		11	9		5		6						2				1			36
	4	3	7		8		12	9		11				5	6					10	2*				1			37
	2	4	7		8		12	10	3	11*				5	6					9					1			38
		2			8		7	9	3	11		4	5	6						10					1			39
		4	2		8		7	9	3	11		12	5*	6						10					1			40
		4	2		8		7	9	3	11	10		5	6											1			41
	2*	4	7		8			9	3	11	10			5	6					12					1			42
	3	4	2		8		7	9		11	10			5	6										1			43
	2	4	3		8		7	9		11	10			5	6										1			44
		4	2		8		7	9		11	10*			5	6*					12	3				1			45
		3			8	7		9	10					5	6*					11	2				1	4	12	46
31	37	29	34	26	27	24	25	34	23	43	25	6	11	25	35	5	6	1		17	19	3	3	2	13	1	1	
					6	6					5		6			1	1		1	2			2				1	
	1		2		1		3	17		14	9		1	2						3								

41

1986-87

1	Aug	23	(a)	Tranmere R	D	1-1	Thomas	2,108
2		30	(h)	Swansea C	W	2-1	Thomas, Williams	4,362
3	Sep	6	(a)	Lincoln C	D	1-1	Thomas	2,305
4		13	(h)	Hereford U	W	2-1	Williams, Thomas (pen)	4,707
5		16	(h)	Halifax T	W	3-2	Clark 3	5,259
6		19	(a)	Scunthopre U	L	0-4		2,689
7		27	(h)	Torquay U	D	1-1	Allardyce	5,053
8		30	(a)	Wolverhampton W	L	0-1		4,409
9	Oct	4	(a)	Burnley	W	4-1	Brazil 2, Thomas 2	5,865
10		11	(h)	Cambridge U	W	1-0	Brazil	5,236
11		18	(h)	Aldershot	L	1-2	Thomas (pen)	5,241
12		20	(a)	Stockport Co	W	3-1	Williams 2, Taylor	2,888
13	Nov	1	(h)	Exeter C	W	2-1	McAteer, Williams	5,818
14		4	(h)	Cardiff C	L	0-1		6,614
15		8	(a)	Northampton T	L	1-3	Taylor	6,537
16		22	(h)	Southend U	W	2-0	Hildersley, Thomas	6,033
17		29	(a)	Peterborough U	L	1-2	Williams	3,462
18	Dec	13	(a)	Colchester U	W	2-0	Williams, Hildersley	2,240
19		20	(h)	Orient	W	1-0	Williams	5,925
20		26	(a)	Crewe Alexandra	D	2-2	Thomas, Atkins	3,784
21		27	(h)	Hartlepool U	D	0-0		7,782
22	Jan	1	(h)	Wrexham	W	1-0	Thomas	9,373
23		3	(a)	Southend U	W	2-1	Bennett, Brazil	4,479
24		17	(a)	Swansea C	D	1-1	Jemson	7,677
25		24	(h)	Lincoln C	W	3-0	Brazil, Swann, Jemson	7,821
26	Feb	7	(a)	Halifax T	W	3-1	Brazil, Swann, Jemson	2,968
27		14	(h)	Scunthorpe U	W	2-1	Brazil, Allardyce	7,968
28		21	(a)	Torquay U	W	2-0	Brazil, Jones	1,871
29		25	(a)	Hereford U	W	3-2	Brazil 2, Worthington	2,628
30		28	(h)	Wolverhampton W	D	2-2	Swann, Worthington	12,592
31	Mar	4	(a)	Exeter C	W	2-1	Brazil (pen), Thomas	5,801
32		14	(a)	Aldershot	D	0-0		3,469
33		17	(h)	Stockport Co	W	3-0	Swann, Worthington, Thomas	7,823
34		21	(a)	Cambridge U	L	0-2		2,804
35		28	(h)	Burnley	W	2-1	Williams, Thomas	10,623
36	Apr	3	(h)	Northampton T	W	1-0	Brazil	16,456
37		7	(a)	Rochdale	W	2-0	Brazil, Zelem	4,986
38		11	(a)	Cardiff C	D	1-1	Thomas	2,528
39		14	(h)	Rochdale	L	2-4	Brazil, Thomas	10,185
40		18	(a)	Wrexham	D	1-1	Williams	4,850
41		20	(h)	Crewe Alexandra	W	2-1	Davis (og), Thomas (pen)	11,107
42		25	(a)	Orient	W	2-1	Brazil, Chapman	5,255
43		28	(h)	Tranmere R	W	2-0	Brazil, Thomas	12,109
44	May	2	(h)	Peterborough U	D	0-0		7,919
45		4	(a)	Hartlepool	D	2-2	Thomas, Brazil	2,617
46		9	(h)	Colchester U	W	1-0	Swann	8,757

FINAL LEAGUE POSITION: 2nd in Division Four

Appearances

Sub. Appearances

Goals

Football appearance/line-up grid (shirt numbers by player and match). Match number is in the right-hand column.

Brown	Bulmer	McAteer	Chapman	Jones	Allardyce	Williams O	Clark	Thomas	Hildsley	Brazil	Bennett	Atkins	McNeil	Kelly	Taylor	Swann	Jemson	Miller	Worthington	Williams P	Zelem	No.
1	2	3	4	5	6	7	8	9	10	11												1
1	2	3	4	5	6	7	8	9	10	11												2
1	2		4	5	6	7	8	9	10	11	3											3
1	2*	3	4	5	6	7	8	9	10	11	12											4
1		3	4	5	6	7	8	9	10	11	2											5
1		3	4*	5	6	7	8	9	10	11	2	12										6
1		3		5	6	7	8	9	10	11	2	4										7
1		3	4	5	6	7	8*	9	10	12	2	11										8
1			8	4	5	7		9	10	11	3	6	2									9
1			8	4	5	7		9	10	11	3	6	2	1								10
			8	5		7	12	9	4*	11	3	6	2	1	10							11
		10	4	5		7				11	3	6	2	1	9							12
1		10	2	5	6	7				11	8	3	4		9							13
1		10	2*	5	6	7	12			11	8	3	4		9							14
1		10		5	6	7	8			11		3	4	2	9							15
1		10	7	5	6			9		11	3	4	2			8						16
1		10*		5	6	7	8	9		11	3	4	2			12						17
1				5	6	7		9	11	10	3	4	2			10						18
1				5	6	7		9	11	10	3	4	2			8						19
1				5	6	7		9	11	10	3	4	2			8						20
1				5	6	7		9	11	10	3	4	2			8						21
1			7	5	6			9	11	10	3	4	2			8						22
1			7	5	6			9	11	10	3	4	2			8						23
1			7	5	6				11	10	3	4	2			8	9					24
1			7	5	6					10	3	4	2	1		8	9	11				25
			7	5	6				12	10	3	4	2	1		8	9*	11				26
			7	5	6				12	10	3	4	2	1		8	9*	11				27
			7	5	6					10	3	4	2	1		8		11	9			28
				5	6	7				10	3	4	2	1		8		11	9			29
			7	5	6				11	10	3	4	2	1		8			9			30
			7	5	6			12	11	10	3	4	2	1		8			9*			31
			7	5	6			9	11	10	3	4	2	1		8						32
			7	5	6*			9	11	10	3	4	2	1		8			12			33
			7	5				9	11	10	3	4	2*	1		3			12	6		34
			7	5		11		9		10	3	4	2	1		8			12	6*		35
			7	5		11		9		10	3	4	2	1		8				6		36
			7	5		11		9		10	3	4		1		8			2	6		37
			7	5		11		9		10	3	4		1		8			2	6		38
			7*	5	6	11		9		10	3	4		1		8			2	12		39
			7	5	6	11		9		10	3	4		1		8			2			40
			7	5	6	11		9		10	3	4		1		8			2			41
			7	5	6	11		9		10	3	4		1		8			2			42
			7*	5	6	11		9		10	3	4		1		8			2	12		43
1				5	6			9	11	10		4				8			2	7	3	44
1		12	5	6				9	11	10		4				8			2	7*	3	45
1			7	5	6			9	11	10	3	4				8			2			46
24	4	16	35	46	37	29	10	35	33	44	41	40	24	22	5	29	4	15	6	1	6	
			1			2	3		1	1	1				1			5				
		1	1	1	2	10		21	2	17	1	1			2	5	3		3		1	

43

1987-88

1	Aug	15	(h)	Chesterfield	L	0-1		6,509
2		22	(a)	Bristol C	L	1-3	Brazil	7,655
3		29	(h)	Wigan Ath	L	0-1		7,057
4	Sep	1	(a)	Southend U	W	2-1	Williams, Atkins	2,600
5		5	(h)	Grimsby T	L	1-3	Swann	5,522
6		12	(a)	York C	D	1-1	Brazil	3,237
7		15	(h)	Northampton T	D	0-0		5,179
8		19	(h)	Rotherham U	D	0-0		5,124
9		26	(a)	Blackpool	L	0-3		8,406
10		29	(h)	Brentford	L	1-2	Lowey	4,241
11	Oct	3	(a)	Walsall	L	0-1		5,467
12		10	(h)	Port Vale	W	3-2	Brazil 2 (1 pen), Ellis	6,274
13		17	(a)	Brighton & HA	D	0-0		6,043
14		20	(h)	Gillingham	D	1-1	Williams	5,676
15		24	(a)	Bury	L	0-4		4,316
16		31	(h)	Chester C	D	1-1	Swann	5,657
17	Nov	4	(a)	Bristol R	W	2-1	Ellis, Jemson	2,804
18		7	(a)	Mansfield T	D	0-0		3,631
19		21	(h)	Doncaster R	L	1-2	Miller	5,178
20		28	(a)	Fulham	W	1-0	Jemson	5,324
21	Dec	12	(h)	Aldershot	L	0-2		4,519
22		19	(a)	Notts Co	L	2-4	Jemson, Swann	5,730
23		26	(h)	Blackpool	W	2-1	Swann, Brazil	11,155
24		28	(a)	Sunderland	D	1-1	Jones	24,814
25	Jan	1	(a)	Wigan Ath	L	0-2		6,872
26		2	(h)	York C	W	3-0	Brazil, Miller, Mooney	6,302
27		9	(h)	Bristol C	W	2-0	Rathbone, Brazil	5,229
28		16	(a)	Rotherham U	D	2-2	Brazil 2	4,011
29		27	(a)	Northampton T	W	1-0	Jemson	5,052
30		30	(h)	Southend U	D	1-1	Mooney	6,180
31	Feb	6	(a)	Grimsby T	W	1-0	Brazil	2,907
32		13	(h)	Sunderland	D	2-2	Swann, Mooney	10,852
33		20	(a)	Chesterfield	D	0-0		2,864
34		27	(h)	Walsall	W	1-0	Brazil (pen)	6,479
35	Mar	1	(a)	Brentford	L	0-2		3,505
36		5	(h)	Brighton & HA	W	3-0	Jemson, Swann 2	5,834
37		12	(a)	Port Vale	L	2-3	Brazil, Swann	4,647
38		19	(a)	Chester C	L	0-1		3,724
39		26	(h)	Bury	W	1-0	Jones	6,456
40	Apr	2	(h)	Mansfield T	W	1-0	Swann	6,254
41		4	(a)	Doncaster R	L	2-3	Swann 2	2,167
42		8	(h)	Bristol R	W	3-1	Ellis, Hildersley, Brazil (pen)	5,386
43		23	(a)	Gillingham	L	0-4		2,721
44		30	(h)	Fulham	W	2-1	Swann, Brazil	4,192
45	May	2	(a)	Aldershot	D	0-0		3,465
46		7	(h)	Notts Co	L	1-2	Ellis	5,822

FINAL LEAGUE POSITION: 16th in Division Three

Appearances

Sub. Appearances

Goals

Kelly	Branagan	Rathbone	Atkins	Chapman	Allardyce	Miller	Swann	Lowey	Brazil	Hildersley	Worthington	Brown	Wrightson	Bennett	Jones	Williams	Jemson	Wilkes	Jeffels	Mooney	Ellis	Joyce	Hughes	No.
1	2	3	4	5	6	7*	8	9	10	11	12													1
	2*	11†	4		6	7	8	9	10		14	1	12	3	5									2
			4	5*	6	2	8		10	11	12	1		3		7	9							3
			4	5	6	2	8		10	11		1		3		7	9							4
			4	5*	6	2	8		10	11	12	1		3		7	9							5
1	11	3	4		6	2	8*		10		14	9†	5			7	12							6
1	2		4		6	7	8		10	11			5	3			9							7
1	2		4		6	7	8		10	11		9	5	3										8
1	2		4		6	7	8			11		9	5	3*			10	12						9
1	2		4	14	6	7†	8*	9		11	12		5	3			10							10
	2		4	11	6		8	9			12	1	5	3			10*			7				11
	2		4		6	7*		14	10		12	1	11	3	5					8†	9			12
	2		4		6				10*	11		1	12	3	5		14			8	9†	7		13
1	2		4		6					11				3	5	7	10				9	8		14
1	2*		4		6					11	12		7	3	5		10				9	8		15
1	2		4		6		8			11				3	5		10			7	9			16
1	2		4		6		8			11				3	5		10			7	9			17
1			4		6	2	8			11				3	5		10			7	9			18
1	2*		4		6	12	8		10	11				3	5		9			7				19
1	2		4		6		8		10	11				3	5		9			7				20
1	2		4		6		8		10	11				3	5		9			7*	12			21
1	2		4		6	12	8		10					3	5*		9			7		11		22
1	2		4		6		8		10		12			3	5		9			7*		11		23
1	2		4		6		8		10	11				3	5					7	9			24
1	2		4	14	6	2	8		10	11				3	5†		12			7	9*			25
			4	5	6	2	8		10			1		3			9			7		11		26
	2*		4	5	6	12	8		10			1		3						7	9	11		27
1	2		4	5	6		8		10					3						7	9	11		28
	2		4		6		8		10			1	5	3			9			7		11		29
	2		4		6		8		10			1	5	3			9			7		11		30
	2		4		6		8		10			1	5	3			9			7		11		31
	2		4		6		8		10			1	5	3			9			7		11		32
	2		4		6		8		10			1	5	3			9*			7	12	11		33
	2		4		6		8		10			1	5	3			9			7		11		34
	2		4		6	12	8		10			1		3*	5		9†			7	14	11		35
	2*		4		6	12	8		10			1		3	5		9			7		11		36
			4		6	2	8		10			1		3	5		9			7		11		37
			4		6	2	8		10			1		3	5	11				7	9			38
		3	4			2	8		10	11		1	6		5					7	9			39
		3	4	12		2	8		10	11		1	6		5*					7	9			40
			4	3*	6	2	8		10	11		1	5						14	7	9†	12		41
		3	4		6	2	8		10	11		1	5							7	9			42
			4		6		8		10	11		1	5			2	12			7	9*	3		43
		3	4		6	2	8		10		12	1	5							7	9*	11		44
		3	4		6	2	8		10†		12	1	5				9			7*	14	11		45
		3	4			2	8					1	5				9			7	10	11	6	46
19	3	36	45	15	38	23	45	4	36	21	4	27	23	34	22	9	24	1	1	34	20	21	1	
				2	1	5	1				4	8		2			1	3	2			4	1	
		1	1			2	12	1	14	1					2	2	5			3	4			

1988-89

#	Month	Date		Opponent		Result	Scorers	Attendance
1	Aug	27	(h)	Port Vale	L	1-3	Williams N	6,718
2	Sep	3	(a)	Huddersfield T	L	0-2		5,622
3		10	(h)	Blackpool	W	1-0	Patterson	8,779
4		17	(a)	Bristol C	D	1-1	Rathbone	7,913
5		20	(h)	Chester C	D	3-3	Patterson 2, Ellis	5,415
6		24	(a)	Notts Co	D	0-0		4,965
7	Oct	1	(h)	Southend U	W	3-2	McAteer, Brazil 2 (1 pen)	5,348
8		5	(a)	Bristol R	L	0-1		3,689
9		8	(h)	Bury	W	1-0	Ellis	5,863
10		15	(a)	Chesterfield	W	3-0	Swann, Mooney, Ellis	2,813
11		22	(a)	Brentford	W	2-0	Brazil 2	5,584
12		25	(h)	Gillingham	W	5-0	Brazil 3 (1 pen), Ellis, Joyce	6,390
13		29	(a)	Swansea C	D	1-1	Ellis	5,370
14	Nov	5	(h)	Mansfield T	W	2-0	Mooney, Rathbone	6,434
15		8	(h)	Wigan Ath	D	2-2	Brazil (pen), Patterson	8,396
16		12	(a)	Reading	D	2-2	Ellis, Patterson	6,225
17		26	(a)	Wolverhampton W	L	0-6		13,180
18	Dec	3	(h)	Cardiff C	D	3-3	Brazil, Ellis 2	4,963
19		17	(a)	Fulham	L	1-2	Patterson	3,858
20		26	(h)	Bolton W	W	3-1	Hughes, Ellis, Joyce	12,104
21		31	(h)	Sheffield U	W	2-0	Patterson, Joyce	11,005
22	Jan	2	(a)	Northampton T	L	0-1		4,219
23		7	(a)	Aldershot	L	1-2	Joyce	2,135
24		14	(h)	Huddersfield T	W	1-0	Patterson	6,959
25		21	(a)	Blackpool	L	0-1		8,951
26		28	(h)	Bristol C	W	2-0	Mooney 2	6,080
27	Feb	3	(a)	Southend U	L	1-2	Mooney	2,948
28		11	(h)	Bristol R	D	1-1	Mooney	7,365
29		18	(a)	Bury	D	1-1	Williams N	6,977
30		25	(h)	Chesterfield	W	6-0	Philliskirk 2, Bloomer (og), Patterson, Ellis 2	7,074
31		28	(a)	Gillingham	W	3-1	Patterson (pen), Ellis 2	3,031
32	Mar	4	(h)	Brentford	W	5-3	Philliskirk, Patterson, Joyce 2, Ellis	8,186
33		11	(a)	Mansfield T	W	3-0	Coleman (og), Philliskirk, Ellis	4,706
34		14	(h)	Swansea C	D	1-1	James (og)	8,975
35		18	(a)	Port Vale	D	1-1	Ellis	8,584
36		25	(h)	Northampton T	W	3-2	Joyce 2, Patterson (pen)	9,137
37		27	(a)	Bolton W	L	0-1		10,281
38	Apr	1	(h)	Fulham	L	1-4	Philliskirk	8,190
39		4	(h)	Aldershot	D	2-2	Bogie, Philliskirk	5,977
40		8	(a)	Sheffield U	L	1-3	Stancliffe (og)	12,718
41		15	(h)	Notts Co	W	3-0	Swann, Joyce, Ellis	6,735
42		22	(a)	Chester C	W	1-0	Jemson	4,617
43		29	(h)	Reading	W	2-1	Patterson 2 (1 pen)	7,003
44	May	1	(a)	Wigan Ath	D	1-1	Jemson	5,671
45		5	(a)	Cardiff C	D	0-0		3,196
46		13	(h)	Wolverhampton W	D	3-3	Ellis 2, Patterson	14,126

FINAL LEAGUE POSITION: 6th in Division Three

Appearances

Sub. Appearances

Goals

Brown	Miller	McAteer	Atkins	Jones	Wrightson	Williams N	Swann	Ellis	Brazil	Patterson	Rathbone	Allardyce	Mooney	Joyce	Hughes	Tunks	Fitzpatrick	Bogie	Philliskirk	Jemson	Harper	
1	2	3	4	5	6	7	8	9	10	11*	12											1
1	2		4	5		9†	8*	14	10	11	3	6	7	12								2
1	7	3	4	5	6			9	10	11	2		8									3
1	7	3	4	5				9	10	11	2	6	8									4
1	7*	3	4	5			12	9	10	11	2	6	8									5
1	7*	3	4	5			8	9	10	11	2	6	12									6
1	12	3	4	5			8	9*	10	11	2	6	7									7
1	2		4	5*	12	14	8†	9	10	11	3	6	7									8
1	2*		4		5	8	12	9		11	3		7	10	6							9
1			4		5	2	10	9		11	3		7	8	6							10
1			4		5	2	10*	9	12	11	3	14	7	8	6†							11
1	11		4	12	5	2		9	10		3	6*	7	8								12
1	12		4		5	2		9	10	11*	3		7	8	6							13
1			4		5	2		9	10	11	3		7	8	6							14
1			4		5	2		9	10	11	3		7	8	6							15
1			4		5	2		9	10	11	3	6	7	8								16
1			4		5*	2		9	10	11	3	6	7	8	12							17
			4			2		9	7	11	3	6		8	5	1	10					18
	3		4	6		2		9		11			7	8	5	1	10					19
	3		4	5		2		9	10	11			7	8	6	1						20
	3		4	5		2		9	10	11			7	8	6	1						21
	12	3†	4	5		2		9*	10	11		14	7	8	6	1						22
	14		4	12		2		9	10	11	3†	5*	7	8	6	1						23
			4	5		2		9	10	11	3		7	8	6	1						24
	12		4	5		2		9	10	11	3*		7	8	6	1						25
		6	4	5		2		9	10	11	3		7	8		1						26
	10*	6	4	5		2		9	12	11	3		7	8		1						27
		6	4	5		2		12		11	3		7	8*		1		9	10			28
		6	4	5		2		8		11	3		7	12		1		9	10*			29
		6	4	5		2		8		11	3		7*	12		1		9	10			30
		6	4	5		2		8		11	3		7			1		9	10			31
		6	4	5		2		8		11	3		7	12		1		9	10*			32
		6	4	5		2		8		11	3		7			1		9	10			33
		6	4	5		2		8		11	3		7	12		1		9*	10			34
		6	4	5		2		8		11	3		7	9		1		12	10*			35
		6	4	5		2		8		11	3		7	9		1			10			36
		6	4	5		2		8		11	3*		7	9		1		12	10†	14		37
		6	4	5		2	11†	8			3		7*	9		1		12	10	14		38
		6	4			2	3	8*		11			7		5	1		9†	10	12	14	39
		6				2	3	8				4	12	9	5	1		7	10*	11		40
1			4	5		2	3	8		11			7	9	6				10			41
1			4	5		2	3	8					7	9	6			12	10	11*		42
1			4	5		2	3	8		11			7	9	6				10			43
1			4	5		2	3	8		11			7	9	6				10*	12		44
1			4	5		2	3	8		11			7	9	6			10*	12			45
1			4	5		2	3	8		11			7	9	6			12	10*			46
23	9	11	39	29	36	40	16	43	23	42	32	13	38	35	22	23	2	9	13	6	2	
	3	2		1	2	1	2	2	2		2	1	2	5	1			4	1	3	3	
		1			2	2	19	9	15	2		6	9	1				1	6	2		

1989-90

1	Aug	19	(a)	Rotherham U	L	1-3	Shaw		5,951
2		26	(h)	Bury	L	2-3	Shaw, Harper		5,622
3	Sep	2	(a)	Leyton Orient	L	1-3	Ellis		4,871
4		9	(h)	Huddersfield T	D	3-3	Bogie, Swann, Mooney		5,822
5		16	(a)	Bristol R	L	0-3			4,350
6		23	(h)	Chester C	W	5-0	Mooney 3, Harper 2 (1 pen)		5,230
7		26	(h)	Blackpool	W	2-1	Bradshaw (og), Atkins		8,920
8		30	(a)	Walsall	L	0-1			4,045
9	Oct	7	(a)	Northampton T	W	2-1	Harper, Ellis		3,039
10		14	(h)	Brentford	W	4-2	Ellis, Joyce, Harper, Swann		5,956
11		17	(h)	Crewe Alex	D	0-0			7,485
12		21	(a)	Notts Co	L	1-2	Williams		5,284
13		28	(h)	Bolton W	L	1-4	Scully		9,135
14		31	(a)	Mansfield T	D	2-2	Mooney, Joyce		3,129
15	Nov	4	(h)	Shrewsbury T	W	2-1	Swann, Patterson		5,418
16		11	(a)	Swansea C	L	1-2	Patterson		3,843
17		25	(a)	Cardiff C	L	0-3			3,270
18	Dec	2	(h)	Reading	W	1-0	Swann		5,067
19		16	(a)	Birmingham C	L	1-3	Patterson (pen)		6,391
20		26	(h)	Tranmere R	D	2-2	Swann 2		8,300
21		30	(h)	Wigan A	D	1-1	Patterson		7,220
22	Jan	1	(a)	Bristol C	L	1-2	Mooney		11,803
23		6	(h)	Fulham	W	1-0	Shaw		5,055
24		13	(a)	Bury	W	2-1	Joyce, Mooney		4,715
25		20	(h)	Rotherham U	L	0-1			6,088
26	Feb	3	(a)	Chester C	L	1-3	Harper		2,499
27		10	(h)	Bristol R	L	0-1			5,956
28		13	(h)	Leyton Orient	L	0-3			4,480
29		17	(a)	Reading	L	0-6			3,998
30		24	(h)	Cardiff C	W	4-0	Harper 3, Joyce		5,716
31	Mar	3	(a)	Fulham	L	1-3	Shaw		4,207
32		6	(h)	Walsall	W	2-0	Swann, Thomas		5,210
33		13	(a)	Blackpool	D	2-2	Shaw, Mooney		8,108
34		17	(h)	Northampton T	D	0-0			5,681
35		20	(a)	Brentford	D	2-2	Joyce, Williams		4,673
36		24	(a)	Crewe Alex	L	0-1			4,531
37		31	(h)	Notts Co	L	2-4	Joyce 2		5,810
38	Apr	3	(a)	Huddersfield T	W	2-0	Joyce, Bogie		4,381
39		7	(a)	Bolton W	L	1-2	Bogie		8,266
40		10	(h)	Mansfield T	W	4-0	Joyce 2, Foster (og), Hughes		5,035
41		14	(h)	Bristol C	D	2-2	Flynn, Harper		7,599
42		16	(a)	Tranmere R	L	1-2	Joyce		10,187
43		21	(h)	Birmingham C	D	2-2	Thomas, Mooney		7,680
44		24	(a)	Wigan A	W	1-0	Thomas		4,454
45		28	(h)	Swansea C	W	2-0	Swann, Williams		6,695
46	May	5	(a)	Shrewsbury T	L	0-2			5,319

FINAL LEAGUE POSITION: 19th in Division Three

Appearances

Sub. Appearances

Goals

Tunks	Miller	Swann	Akins	Jones	Hughes	Mooney	Ellis	Joyce	Shaw	Patterson	Rathbone	Wrightson	Snow	Harper	Kelly	Bogie	Williams	Scully	Bennett	Flynn	Greenwood	Stowell	McLroy	Thomas	Anderton	
1	2	3	4	5	6	7	8	9	10	11																1
1	11	3	4	5		7		9	10		2	6	8*	12												2
	2*	11	4	5		7	8	9	10		3	6			1	12										3
		3			6	7	8*	9	10		12	4			1	11	2	5								4
		3*	14		6	7	8	9	10		12	4†			1	11	2	5								5
		3	4		6	7	8	9						10	1	11	2	5								6
		3	4		6	7	8	9						10	1	11	2	5								7
		3	4		6	7*	8	9	12					10	1	11	2	5								8
		3	4		6	7	8	9	12					10	1	11*	2	5								9
		3	4			7	8	9				6		10	1	11	2	5								10
		3	4		6	7	8	9						10	1	11	2	5								11
		3	4		6	7	8	9	12					10*	1	11	2	5								12
		3	4		6*	7	8	9	12					10	1	11	2	5								13
		3	4		6	7	8*	5	10	9				12	1	11	2									14
		3	4			7*		5	10	9	12			8	1	11	2	6								15
		3	4		14		8	5	10*	11	12			7†	1	9	2	6								16
		3	4		14	7	8	5	10*	11				12	1	9	2	6†								17
		3	4		6	7	8	5	10	11					1	9	2									18
		9†	4		6*		12	8	10	14	7			11	1		2		3		5					19
		8	4		6	7		9	10					11	1	4	2		3		5					20
		8			6	7		9	10					11	1	4	2		3		5					21
		8			6	7		9	10					11	1	4	2		3		5					22
		8			6	7		9	11	10					1	4	2		3		5					23
			4			7		9	10	8		6		11	1		2		3	5						24
			4		6	7		9*	10	8				11	1	12	2		3	5						25
			4		6*	7		9	10	8				12	1		2		3	5	11					26
		3				7		9	10			6		11			2		8	5		1	4			27
		2				7		9	10*			6		11		12	3		8	5		1	4			28
		2			6	7		9				4			1	11	3		8	5			10			29
		3				7		9		8		6		11	1		2			5			4	10		30
		3			6	7				8		5		11	1	9	2			5			4	10		31
		3			6	7			10	8		5		11	1		2						4	9		32
		3			6	7			5	8		4			1		2			10	11			9		33
		3				7			10	8		6		11	1		2			5			4	9		34
		3	11*		8	7			10	14		6		12	1		2			5			4	9†		35
		3	11*		8†	7			10	9		6		12	1	14	2			5			4			36
		3			12	7		9*	10†			6		11	1	14	2			5	8		4			37
		3	10		8	7		9				6			1	11	2			5			4			38
		3	10		8	7		9				6			1	11	2			5			4			39
		3	10		8	7		9*				6		12	1	11	2			5			4†	14		40
		3	10*		8	7		9				6		12	1	11	2			5			4			41
		3	10		12	7†		8		14		6			1	11	2			5*			4	9		42
		3			12	7		8		14		6		11†	1	10	2			5*			4	9		43
		3	5			7		8				6		11	1	10	2						4	9		44
		3	5			7		8				6		11	1	10	2						4	9		45
		3	5		12	7		8		14		6		11†	1	10	2						4*	9		46
2	3	46	27	3	29	44	17	44	24	12	3	26	1	28	42	30	41	13	10	23	5	2	20	11		
			1		6	1			7	1	5			8		5								1		
		8	1		1	9	3	11	5	4				10		3	3	1		1			3			

49

1990-91

1	Aug	25	(h)	Grimsby T	L	1-3	Joyce		6,372
2	Sep	1	(a)	Reading	D	3-3	Joyce, Peel, Senior		4,228
3		8	(h)	Tranmere R	L	0-4			5,648
4		14	(a)	Southend U	L	2-3	Joyce, Thomas (pen)		4,614
5		18	(a)	Bolton W	W	2-1	James, Bogie (pen)		5,844
6		22	(h)	Fulham	W	1-0	Hughes		4,691
7		29	(a)	Birmingham C	D	1-1	Bogie		7,154
8	Oct	2	(h)	Brentford	D	1-1	Swann		5,025
9		6	(h)	Exeter C	W	1-0	Bogie		4,716
10		13	(a)	Mansfield T	W	1-0	Rathbone		3,225
11		20	(a)	Rotherham U	L	0-1			4,599
12		23	(h)	Chester C	D	0-0			5,465
13		27	(h)	Bournemouth	D	0-0			4,953
14	Nov	3	(a)	Wigan A	L	1-2	Greenwood		4,728
15		10	(a)	Bradford C	L	1-2	Bogie		7,440
16		24	(h)	Huddersfield T	D	1-1	Joyce		4,646
17	Dec	1	(h)	Shrewsbury T	W	4-3	Bogie 2, Wrightson, Swann		4,515
18		15	(a)	Leyton Orient	L	0-1			3,282
19		22	(h)	Stoke C	W	2-0	Swann 2		7,532
20		26	(a)	Crewe Alex	D	2-2	Bogie, Shaw		4,405
21		29	(a)	Bury	L	1-3	Mooney		5,404
22	Jan	1	(h)	Cambridge U	L	0-2			5,256
23		12	(h)	Reading	L	1-2	Swann		4,470
24		19	(a)	Grimsby T	L	1-4	Mooney		5,391
25		26	(h)	Southend U	W	2-1	Shaw, Wrightson		4,351
26	Feb	2	(h)	Bolton W	L	1-2	Wrightson		9,844
27		5	(a)	Fulham	L	0-1			2,750
28		16	(a)	Huddersfield T	L	0-1			5,504
29		23	(h)	Bradford C	L	0-3			6,878
30	Mar	2	(a)	Shrewsbury T	W	1-0	Shaw		2,989
31		9	(h)	Leyton Orient	W	2-1	Shaw, Thompson		3,651
32		12	(a)	Brentford	L	0-2			4,856
33		16	(h)	Birmingham C	W	2-0	Cartwright, Joyce		5,334
34		19	(h)	Mansfield T	W	3-1	Jepson 2, Joyce (pen)		3,245
35		23	(a)	Exeter C	L	0-4			3,525
36		26	(h)	Swansea C	W	2-0	Shaw 2		3,491
37		30	(h)	Crewe Alex	W	5-1	Joyce, Shaw, Bogie, Thompson, James		4,852
38	Apr	1	(a)	Stoke C	W	1-0	Shaw		11,524
39		6	(h)	Bury	D	1-1	Shaw		5,641
40		13	(a)	Cambridge U	D	1-1	Joyce		6,262
41		16	(a)	Swansea C	L	1-3	Senior		2,507
42		20	(h)	Rotherham U	L	1-2	Flynn		4,069
43		27	(a)	Chester C	D	1-1	Joyce		1,351
44	May	2	(a)	Bournemouth	D	0-0			7,064
45		7	(a)	Tranmere R	L	1-2	Ashcroft		6,006
46		11	(h)	Wigan A	W	2-1	Jepson, Shaw		5,917

FINAL LEAGUE POSITION: 17th in Division Three

Appearances

Sub. Appearances

Goals

Farnworth	Senior	Swann	Greaves	Flynn	Wrightson	Williams	Joyce	Thomas	Shaw	Harper	Peel	Bogie	James	Hughes	Kelly	Fee	Rathbone	Greenwood	Ashcroft	Mooney	Easter	Thompson	Jepson	Cartwright	Lambert	Eaves	Kerfoot	Jackson		
1	2	3	4	5	6	7	8	9	10	11*	12																			1
1	2	3		5	6	7*	10	9		12	8†	4	11	14																2
1	2	3			6	7	10	9		8*	12	4	11	5																3
	2*	8			6	3	11	9	10			7	12	5	1	4														4
1		11			6	2	7	9*	10	12		8	3	5		4														5
1		10			6	2	7		9			8	11	5		4	3													6
1	2	11			6	7	10		9			8	3	5*		4	12													7
1	2	11			6	7*	10		9	12		8	3	5		4														8
1	2	11			6		10		9			8	7	5		4	3													9
1	2	11			6	14*	10		9	12		8	7	5†		4	3													10
1	2	11	12		6		10		9	7*		8	3	5		4														11
1		11	2	5	6		10		7			8	3	9*		4			12											12
1		11		2	6		10		7			8	3	5		4			9											13
1	2	11		4	6		10		7	8*			3	5†			12		9	14										14
	2	7*		4	6		11		10	12		8	14	5	1		3		9											15
	2	10			6		4		9	7*	12	8	11	5	1		3													16
	2	10			6		4		9	11		8		5	1		3			7										17
	2	10	12		6	14	4		9	11		8		5	1		3†			7*										18
	2	11		4	6	3	9		10			8		5	1					7										19
	2	11		4	6	3	9		10			8		5	1					7										20
	2	11		4	6	3†	9		10	12	14	8		5*	1					7										21
	2	11		4	6		9		10	12	14	8†		5*	1		3			7										22
	2	11		4	6		9		10*	14					1	5	3	12		7	8									23
	2	11		4	6		9		10	8					1	5	3			7										24
		11		4	6		9		10	8		3			1	5	2			7										25
1		11		5	6		2		10	8	12	3				4			9			7*								26
1		11		5	6		2		10	8*	12	3				4			9			7								27
1	2	11		5	6		3		10	8†	12	14	4									7*	9							28
1		11		5	6		3		10	8*		2	4						12			7	9							29
1	2	11		5	6				10			3	4									7	9	8						30
1	2			5	6				10	12		3	4						11			7	9*	8						31
1	2			5					10	11		4	6†						12			7		8	3*	9	14			32
1	2			5	6	4			10	11		3										7	9	8						33
1	2			5	6	4			10	11		3										7	9	8						34
1	2			5	6	4			10	11	8†	3							12			7*	9		14					35
	2			5	6	4			10	11		8	3		1							7	9							36
	2			5	6†	4			10*	11		8	3		1							7	9	12			14			37
	2			5	6	4			10	11		8	3		1				12			7*	9							38
	2				6	4			10	11		8	3		1				12			7*	9				5			39
	2			6		4			10	11		3			1							7	9	8			5			40
	2			6		4			10	11	12	3			1							7	9	8*	14		5†			41
	2			6	5	4			10*	11		8	3		1				12			7	9							42
	2			6	5	4			10†	11		12	3		1				14			7*	9	8						43
	2			5		4			10	11		3			1				9			7		8	6					44
	2			5		4			10*	11	14	12	3		1				9†			7		8	6					45
	2			5					10	11	8†	3			1				9*			7	12	4	6	14				46
22	38	30	2	33	40	11	42	5	44	27	1	28	34	25	23	15	11	3	6	9	1	21	13	13	4	1		3		
			2		2				9	9		3	3	1			2	2	8				1	1	1	2	1	1		
	2	5		1	3		9	1	10	1		8	2	1		1	1			1		2	2	3	1					

51

1991-92

#	Month	Date		Opponent	Result	Score	Scorers	Attendance
1	Aug	17	(a)	Peterbrough U	L	0-1		6,036
2		24	(h)	Torquay U	W	3-0	Shaw, Ashcroft, Greenwood	3,654
3		30	(a)	Stockport Co	L	0-2		5,405
4	Sep	3	(h)	Bournemouth	D	2-2	James M, Greenwood	3,170
5		7	(h)	Bradford C	D	1-1	Joyce (pen)	4,160
6		14	(a)	Swansea C	D	2-2	Shaw 2	3,170
7		17	(a)	Leyton Orient	D	0-0		3,296
8		21	(h)	Stoke C	D	2-2	Jepson, Swann	6,345
9		28	(a)	Birmingham C	L	1-3	Shaw	8,760
10	Oct	1	(h)	West Brom A	W	2-0	Swann, Senior	5,293
11		12	(a)	Bury	W	3-2	Ashcroft, Greenwood, Shaw	4,265
12		19	(h)	Huddersfield T	W	1-0	James M	6,866
13		26	(a)	Fulham	L	0-1		4,022
14	Nov	2	(a)	Chester C	L	2-3	Shaw, Swann	1,219
15		5	(h)	Wigan A	W	3-0	Swann, Joyce 2 (1 pen)	3,657
16		9	(h)	Darlington	W	2-1	Thomas, Shaw	4,643
17		23	(a)	Bolton W	L	0-1		7,033
18		30	(a)	Hull C	D	2-2	Thomas, Shaw	4,280
19	Dec	14	(h)	Hartlepool U	L	1-4	Ashcroft	5,032
20		20	(a)	Torquay U	L	0-1		2,183
21		26	(h)	Stockport Co	W	3-2	Swann, Shaw (pen), James M	6,782
22		28	(h)	Peterbrough U	D	1-1	Cartwright	5,200
23	Jan	1	(a)	Bournemouth	L	0-1		5,508
24		11	(a)	Shrewsbury T	L	0-2		3,154
25		18	(h)	Exeter C	L	1-3	Lambert	3,585
26		25	(a)	Brentford	L	0-1	.	7,559
27	Feb	1	(a)	Huddersfield T	W	2-1	Shaw, Cartwright	6,700
28		8	(h)	Fulham	L	1-2	Johnrose	3,878
29		11	(h)	Hull C	W	3-1	Williams, Jepson 2	2,932
30		15	(a)	Hartlepool U	L	0-2		2,140
31		22	(h)	Shrewsbury T	D	2-2	James M, Wrightson	3,342
32		29	(a)	Reading	D	2-2	Lambert, Shaw	3,390
33	Mar	3	(a)	Exeter C	L	1-4	Ashcroft	2,214
34		7	(h)	Brentford	W	3-2	Shaw, Thompson, Ashcroft	3,548
35		10	(a)	Wigan A	L	0-3		3,364
36		14	(h)	Chester C	L	0-3		3,909
37		21	(a)	Darlington	W	2-0	Jepson 2	2,270
38		28	(h)	Bolton W	W	2-1	Joyce (pen), Flynn	7,327
39		31	(h)	Swansea C	D	1-1	Greenall	3,367
40	Apr	4	(a)	Bradford C	D	1-1	Shaw	6,044
41		11	(h)	Leyton Orient	W	2-1	Flynn, Howard (og)	3,926
42		14	(h)	Reading	D	1-1	Cartwright	3,203
43		18	(a)	Stoke C	L	1-2	Thompson	16,151
44		24	(h)	Birmingham C	W	3-2	Cartwright, Flynn, Shaw	7,738
45		25	(a)	West Brom A	L	0-3		11,318
46	May	2	(h)	Bury	W	2-0	Joyce, Finney	6,932

FINAL LEAGUE POSITION: 17th in Division Three

Appearances

Sub. Appearances

Goals

Franworth	Senior	Swann	Wrightson	Flynn	Berry	Thompson	Joyce	Jepson	Shaw	James M	Williams	Aschroft	Greenwood	Lambert	Kelly	James	Cartwright	Cross	Thomas	Allpress	Hughes	Kerfoot	Ainsworth	Whitworth	Finney	Johnrose	Greenall	Christie	
1	2	3	4	5	6	7	8	9	10	11																			1
1	2	4	6	5			8	9*	10	3	7	11	12																2
1	2	8*	6	5	7			9	10	3	12	14	11	4†															3
	2	8	3	5	6	7*	4	9	10	11			12		1														4
	2	4	3	5	6*		8	9	10	11		12	7		1														5
	2	4	3	5		12		9	10	11				7	1	6	8*												6
	2	11	6	5		12	8	9	10†	3				7*	1	4	14												7
	2	4	3	5		12	8	9	10	11				7*	1	6													8
	2	4	7	5			8	9	10*	11					1	6		3	12										9
	2	4	7	5			8		10	11			9		1	6		3											10
	2†	4	7	5		12	8		10		14	11	9		1	6		3*											11
	2	4	6	5		12	8		10		11	7	9*		1			3											12
	2	4	6	5		12	8		10		14	7			1		11	3†	9*										13
	2*	4	3	5		9	8		10	11†	14	7			1		12				6								14
		4	3	5		9	8		10	11	2	7			1						6								15
	2	4*	3	5		9†	8		10	11	14	7			1					12	6								16
	2	4	3†	5			8*		10	11	14	7	12		1				9		6								17
	2	4	3	5					10	11		7	12		1		8		9*		6								18
	2	4	3	5					10			7	11*	14	1		8		9	6†	12								19
	2								10			7	11	6*	1		8		9	12	4								20
	2	4	3	5*					10	11		7	9		1		8			12	6								21
	2	4	3	5					10	11		7	9*		1		8		12		6								22
	2	4	3	5				12	10†			7			1		8		9	11*	6	14							23
1	2	4	3	5					10*			7					8		9		6	12	11						24
1	2	4	3*						10†			7	12				8		9		6		11	5	14				25
1	2	4						12		11		7	10	3			8				6			5		9*			26
1	2†	4		3					10*	11		7	9	14			8				6		12	5					27
1	2	11	3	5					10		12	7*	9				8			4†				6		14			28
1	2		4	5			9*		10		11	7		3			8							6		12			29
1	2		4	5					10		11	7	9	3			8							6					30
	2		4	5				9	10	3	11	7			1		8				6								31
	2	14	4	5				9	10	11	7*	12		3	1		8				6†								32
	2	8	6	5			14	9†	10	11	12	7		3*	1		4												33
1	2		3	5			9*	8		10	11	12	7				4				6								34
1	2		3	5			9	8		10	11	7		12			4*				6								35
1			3	5			9	8	12	10	11	2*	7				4				6								36
1		6		5				11	8	9	10	3	2	7			4												37
1				5				11	8	9	10	3	2	7			4										6		38
1				5				11	8	9	10*	3	2	7			4							12			6		39
1	7*			5				11	8	9	10	3	2				4							12			6		40
1				5				11	8	9	10	3	2	7*			4										6	12	41
1		5						11	8	9	10	3	2	7			4										6		42
1				5			9*	11	8		10	3	2	7			4										6	12	43
1				5				11	8	9	10	3	2	7			4										6		44
1		12		5				11*	8	9†	10	3	2	7			4						14				6		45
1				5				11	8	9*	10	3	2	7			4							12			6		46
23	35	28	36	43	4	18	28	23	45	36	17	35	16	7	23	6	31	5	8	7	14	2	6	1	9				
		1	1			7	1	1	1			9	3	4	4		2		3	2	1	3	3		2	2		2	
	1	5	1	3		2	5	5	14	4	1	5	3	2		4		2					1	1	1				

53

1992-93

1	Aug	15	(h)	Bournemouth	D	1-1	Ellis	4,756
2		22	(a)	Fulham	L	1-2	Ellis	3,641
3		29	(h)	Chester C	W	4-3	Cartwright, Flynn, Ashcroft, Leonard	4,471
4	Sep	5	(a)	Brighton & HA	L	0-2		6,026
5		12	(h)	Burley	W	2-0	Tinker, Ashcroft	7,209
6		15	(a)	Hull C	W	4-2	Ellis 2, Ashcroft, Cartwright	4,463
7		19	(a)	Bradford C	L	0-4		5,882
8		26	(h)	Hartlepool U	L	0-2		4,347
9	Oct	3	(h)	Plymouth A	L	1-2	Davidson	4,401
10		10	(a)	Blackpool	W	3-2	Ellis 3	7,631
11		17	(h)	Stoke C	L	1-2	Callaghan	8,138
12		20	(h)	Reading	W	2-0	Flitcroft, Ashcroft (pen)	3,329
13		24	(a)	Mansfield T	D	2-2	James, Fowler L	3,047
14		31	(h)	Bolton W	D	2-2	James, Cartwright	7,013
15	Nov	3	(a)	Stockport C	L	0-3		4,860
16		7	(h)	Wigan A	W	2-0	Callaghan, James	4,442
17		21	(a)	Rotherham U	L	0-1		4,246
18		28	(h)	West Brom A	D	1-1	Ellis	6,306
19	Dec	12	(h)	Port Vale	L	2-5	James, Ashcroft (pen)	6,038
20		18	(a)	Leyton Orient	L	1-3	Ashcroft	3,436
21		28	(h)	Exeter C	D	2-2	Garnett, Norbury	5,796
22	Jan	9	(h)	Hull C	L	1-2	Garnett	4,719
23		16	(a)	Hartlepool U	D	0-0		2,682
24		23	(h)	Bradford C	W	3-2	Norbury, James, Ellis	5,155
25		26	(a)	Chester C	W	4-2	Norbury, Flynn, Ellis, Flitcroft	2,901
26		30	(h)	Fulham	L	1-2	Ellis	5,858
27	Feb	6	(a)	Bournemouth	L	1-2	Tinker	3,601
28		13	(h)	Brighton & HA	W	1-0	Norbury	4,334
29		16	(a)	Burnley	L	0-2		12,648
30		20	(a)	Reading	L	0-4		3,543
31		27	(h)	Blackpool	D	3-3	Ellis 2, Fowler L	10,403
32	Mar	6	(a)	Plymouth A	L	0-4		5,201
33		9	(h)	Swansea C	L	1-3	Norbury	4,396
34		12	(a)	Wigan A	W	3-2	Norbury, Burton 2	3,562
35		17	(a)	Huddersfield T	L	0-1		4,915
36		20	(h)	Stockport C	L	2-3	Ellis 2	5,255
37		24	(a)	West Brom A	L	2-3	Ellis, Ashcroft	13,270
38		27	(h)	Rotherham U	W	5-2	Norbury 2, Ellis 3	4,859
39	Apr	6	(a)	Port Vale	D	2-2	Ellis, Watson	8,271
40		10	(h)	Huddersfield T	W	2-1	Watson, Ellis	7,647
41		12	(a)	Exeter C	W	1-0	Watson	3,410
42		17	(h)	Leyton Orient	L	1-4	Burton	5,890
43		24	(a)	Stoke C	L	0-1		18,334
44		27	(a)	Swansea C	L	0-2		6,933
45	May	1	(h)	Mansfield T	L	1-5	Ellis	5,889
46		8	(a)	Bolton W	L	0-1		21,270

FINAL LEAGUE POSITION: 21st in Division Two

Appearances

Sub. Appearances

Goals

Farnworth	Davidson	Fowler L	Tinkler	Flynn	Callaghan	Ashcroft	Cartwright	Leonard	Ellis	James	Eaves	Flitcroft	Christie	Burton	Finney	Kidd	Graham	Allardyce	Taylor	Siddall	Garnett	Moylon	Lucas	Ainsworth	Norbury	Johnstone	Greenall	Fowler J	Whalley	Watson	Allardyce	
1	2	3	4	5	6	7	8	9	10	11																						1
1	2	3	4*	5	6	7	8	9	10	11†	12	14																				2
1	2	3	4†	5	6	7	8	9	10	11*			14	12																		3
1	2	3		5	6	7	8	9	10*	14	4	11†	12																			4
1	2	3	4	5	6†	7	8	9	10*	11	14			12																		5
1	2	3	4	5	6	7	8	9	10	11																						6
1	2	3	4*	5	6	7	8	9	10	11					12																	7
1	2	3	4	5	6*	7	8	9	10	11		12																				8
1	2	3	4	5	6	7	8	9	10	11																						9
1	2	3†	4	5	6	7	8	9	10*	11						12	14															10
1	2	3	4	5	6	7	8	9	10	11*						12																11
1	12	3	4	5	11	7	2	9	10			8*				6																12
1	12	3	4	5	10	7	2	9*		11						6†	8	14														13
1	12	3	4	5	8		2		10	11						6*	7		9													14
1	3	6	4	5	8		2†		10	11	12						7*	14	9													15
1	3	6	5	4	7		2		10	11							8		9													16
1	3	6	5	4	7		2			11				12			8	9	10*													17
1	3	6	7	5	4	9	2		10	11							8															18
	2	3	5	4	9				10	11		8					7			1	6											19
1	3	2†	5	4	12				10	11		8		9			7*				6			14								20
1	2		5	4	7				10	11											6		3	8	9							21
1	12	2	5	4	7					11				10*							6		3	8	9							22
1	11		5	4	7		2		10												6		3	8	9							23
1	2		5	4	7				10	11											6		3	8	9							24
1*	2		5†	4	7				10	11		14		12							6		3	8	9							25
	12	4*			7		2		10	11				5							6		3	8	9		1					26
	11*	4			7		2		10												6		3	8	9		1	5				27
	12	2	5		7				10	11*											6		3	8	9		1	4				28
	3	2	5				12	7	14	10				11*									4	8	9		1		6			29
	3		5			2	12	11†	14	10				8*									4		9		1		6	7		30
	8		5				4		10	11													3	2	9		1		6	7		31
			5†				12	7*	10	11			14										3	2	9		1		6	8	4	32
1	7		5						10	11													3	2	9		1		6	8	4	33
	7		5						10	11				12									3	2		9*	1		6	8	4	34
	7*		5			8			10	11				12									3	2	9		1		6		4	35
			5			8		7	10	11													3	2	9		1		6		4	36
1			5			8		7	10	11													3	2	9		1		6		4	37
1							11	7	10					8		5							3	2	9				6		4	38
1*							11	7	10					8†		5							3	2			6	12	4	9	14	39
1							11	7	10					8		5							3	2			6		4	9		40
1	12						11	7	10*					8		5							3	2			6		4	9		41
1							11	7	10					8		5							3	2			6		4	9		42
1	12						2	7*	10	11				8									3	4			6			9		43
1							2		10*	11	14		14	8		5							3	7	9		6†		4	12		44
1	3								10*	11				12		5							7	2	9		6		4	8		45
1	7*						2		10	11						5							3	8	9		6		4	12		46
35	18	29	22	35	33	37	33	19	34	22	1	4	1	17	1	13	8	1	4	1	10		26	26	21	10	20	5	14	6		
	3	3	2		2	2	1	3	1	3	3		4	1	4	3	2		2	1					1				2	1		
	1	2	2	2	2	7	3	1	22	5		2		3							2				8				3	1		

1993-94

1	Aug	14	(h)	Crewe Alex	L	0-2		6,879
2		21	(a)	Scarborough	W	4-3	Ellis 2, Ainsworth 2	2,329
3		28	(h)	Shrewsbury T	W	6-1	Ainsworth 2, Conroy 3, Nebbeling	4,941
4		31	(h)	Bury	W	3-1	Nebbeling, Conroy, Ellis	5,886
5	Sep	4	(a)	Lincoln C	W	2-0	Ellis, Raynor	3,793
6		11	(h)	Doncaster R	W	3-1	Conroy, Matthewson, Raynor	7,294
7		18	(a)	Torquay U	L	3-4	Conroy, Ellis, Ainsworth	3,912
8		25	(a)	Mansfield T	D	2-2	Ellis 2	3,762
9	Oct	2	(h)	Colchester U	W	1-0	Ellis	6,412
10		9	(h)	Chesterfield	W	4-1	Raynor, Ellis 3 (1 pen)	6,581
11		16	(a)	Wigan A	D	2-2	Conroy, Challender	3,741
12		23	(h)	Rochdale	W	2-1	Ellis 2 (1 pen)	8,491
13		30	(a)	Hereford U	W	3-2	Moyes, Ellis 2	3,383
14	Nov	2	(a)	Walsall	L	0-2		4,446
15		6	(h)	Darlington	W	3-2	Nebbeling 2, Cartwright	6,711
16		20	(a)	Carlisle U	W	1-0	Ellis	10,279
17		27	(h)	Wycombe W	L	2-3	Ainsworth, Challender	9,265
18	Dec	11	(h)	Scarborough	D	2-2	Bryson, Ellis (pen)	6,290
19		17	(a)	Crewe Alex	L	3-4	Moyes, Conroy, Raynor	6,035
20		27	(h)	Chester C	D	1-1	Ellis	12,790
21	Jan	1	(h)	Scunthorpe U	D	2-2	Conroy, Norbury	7,669
22		4	(a)	Bury	D	1-1	Norbury	4,164
23		15	(h)	Wigan A	W	3-0	Ellis 2, Conroy	7,728
24		22	(a)	Chesterfield	D	1-1	Moyes	3,804
25	Feb	5	(a)	Rochdale	L	1-2	Conroy	4,317
26		12	(h)	Gillingham	D	0-0		6,167
27		19	(a)	Shrewsbury T	L	0-1		5,391
28		25	(h)	Lincoln C	W	2-0	Conroy, Raynor	5,941
29	Mar	1	(h)	Hereford U	W	3-0	Ellis 2, Bryson	6,641
30		4	(a)	Doncaster R	D	1-1	Yates (og)	3,321
31		12	(h)	Torquay U	W	3-1	Ellis 2, Sulley	6,641
32		15	(a)	Northampton T	L	0-2		3,845
33		19	(h)	Mansfield T	W	3-1	Norbury 2, Ainsworth	6,747
34		26	(a)	Colchester U	D	1-1	Norbury	2,950
35	Apr	2	(a)	Chester C	L	2-3	Ainsworth, Ellis	5,638
36		4	(h)	Northampton T	D	1-1	Ainsworth	7,517
37		9	(a)	Scunthorpe U	L	1-3	Ainsworth, Ellis	3,790
38		12	(a)	Gillingham	D	2-2	Moyes, Green (og)	2,453
39		16	(h)	Walsall	W	2-0	Ainsworth, Fensome	7,020
40		23	(a)	Darlington	W	2-0	Raynor, Ellis	2,739
41		30	(h)	Carlisle U	L	0-3		11,363
42	May	7	(a)	Wycombe W	D	1-1	Kidd	7,442

FINAL LEAGUE POSITION: 5th in Division Three

Appearances

Sub. Appearances

Goals

O'Hanlon	Callaghan	Sulley	Nebbeling	Kidd	Raynor	Ainsworth	Whalley	Norbury	Ellis	Burton	Masefield	Cartwright	Conroy	Matthewson	Lucas	Moyes	Bamber	Challender	Woods	Fensome	Holland	Bryson	Watson	Magee	Kibane	Hicks	Squires	
1	2	3	4	5	6	7	8	9	10	11																		1
1		3	4	5	6	7	11	9*	10		2	8	12															2
1		3	5		11	7	4	12	10*		2	8	9	6														3
1		3	5		11	7	4		10		2	8		6														4
1		3	5	12	11	7	4		10		2*	8	9	6														5
1		3	5	2	11	7	4		10			8	9	6														6
1		3	5	2†	11	7	4	12	10			8	9*	6	14													7
1			5		11	7	4		10			8	9*	6	3	2	12											8
1		3	5		11	7		12	10		2	8	9*	6	4†			14										9
		3	5		11	7			10		2	8	9	6*	4				1									10
		5	3		11	7			10			8	9	6*	4				1	2	12							11
1		5	3		11	7†	4	12	10			8	9*	6				14		2								12
1		5	3		11		4	9	10			8	7	6						2								13
1		5	3		11		4†	9*	10		12	8	7	6				14		2								14
1		5	3		11		4	12	10*			8	9		7	6				2								15
1		5	3		11	7*		12	10			8	9		4	6				2								16
1*			3		11	7	4		10				9		5	6		8	12	2								17
			3		11	7	4	12	10				9*		5	6		8†	1	2		14						18
1		3	5		11	7	4		10*				14	12	8	6		2†				9						19
1		5	3		11	7*	4†		10				14	12	8	6				2		9						20
1		5	3		11			12	10*				4	9	8	6				2		7						21
1		5	3		11	7*		12	10				4	9	8	6				2		10						22
1		3	5		11*			12	10			8	9		4	6				2		7						23
1		5	3		11*			12	10			8	9		4	6				2		7						24
		5†	3		11*		14	12	10			8	9		4	6			1	2		7						25
		3	5		11*		14	12	10			8†	9		4	6			1	2		7						26
			5		11		3	9	10*			8	12		4	6			1	2		7						27
		3	5		11	7		12	10				9		4*	6			1	2		8						28
		3	5		11	7			10				4	9		6			1	2		8						29
			3	12		7*	14						4	9	5	6			1	2		8	10	11†				30
			3	2	11	7		9*	10				4		5	6			1			8			12			31
			3	11†		7		12	10				9		5*	6			1	2		8		14				32
1		3	5		11	7							9		4	6				2		8						33
1		3	5	12		7							9		4	6		10		2		8		11*				34
			3		11	7		9	10				4	6					1	2		8				5		35
			3			7		9	10				4	6					1	2	12	8		11		5*		36
			3			7	14	9†	10				4	6					1	2	12	8		11		5*		37
			3	5		7			10				9		4	6			1	2		8		11	12			38
			5	12		7		9*	10						4	6			1	2		8		11			3	39
			5	10†		7		12					9*		4	6		14	1	2		8		11			3	40
			5	9		7			10						4	6			1	2		8		11			3	41
			5	9		7									4	6		14	1	2		8	10	11†			3*	42
23	1	21	22	32	36	34	17	11	36	2	6	36	27	12	21	29		5	19	31		24	1	5		3	1	
			3	4	4	10	1	1				3	4		3			1	5	1		1	1	2	1	1		
		1	4	1		6	11		5	26		1	12	1		4			2			1		2				

1994-95

1	Aug	13	(a)	Darlington	D	0-0		3,800
2		20	(a)	Hereford U	W	2-0	Conroy, Sale	3,039
3		27	(a)	Barnet	L	1-2	Sale	2,441
4		30	(a)	Bury	D	0-0		3,623
5	Sep	3	(h)	Lincoln C	W	4-0	Moyes, Sale 2, Ainsworth	8,337
6		10	(a)	Fulham	W	1-0	Trebble	5,001
7		13	(a)	Gillingham	W	3-2	Sale 2, Fleming	2,555
8		17	(h)	Darlington	L	1-3	Trebble	8,884
9		24	(a)	Doncaster R	L	1-2	Fleming	3,321
10	Oct	1	(h)	Walsall	L	1-2	Whalley	7,852
11		8	(h)	Scunthorpe U	L	0-1		6,895
12		15	(a)	Hartlepool U	L	1-3	Atkinson	2,002
13		22	(a)	Colchester U	L	1-3	Trebble	3,015
14		29	(h)	Exeter C	L	0-1		6,808
15	Nov	5	(a)	Mansfield T	W	2-1	Conroy 2	2,602
16		19	(h)	Northampton T	W	2-0	Moyes, Raynor	7,297
17		26	(a)	Chesterfield	L	0-1		3,191
18	Dec	10	(h)	Hereford U	W	4-2	Magee, Conroy, Bryson 2 (2 pen)	6,581
19		17	(h)	Barnet	W	1-0	Kidd	6,429
20		26	(h)	Rochdale	W	3-0	Smart, Kidd, Conroy	10,491
21		31	(h)	Scarborough	W	1-0	Smart	8,407
22	Jan	2	(a)	Torquay U	L	0-1		3,770
23		10	(h)	Colchester U	W	2-1	Smart, Trebble	6,377
24		17	(a)	Carlisle U	D	0-0		10,684
25		21	(h)	Mansfield T	W	2-1	Bryson, Smart	8,448
26		24	(a)	Wigan A	D	1-1	Cartwright	3,618
27	Feb	4	(h)	Chesterfield	D	0-0		8,544
28		11	(a)	Northampton T	L	1-2	Smart	5,195
29		18	(h)	Carlisle U	W	1-0	Conroy	11,897
30		28	(a)	Walsall	D	2-2	Conroy, Raynor	4,492
31	Mar	4	(h)	Doncaster R	D	2-2	Davey, Beckham	9,624
32		11	(h)	Fulham	W	3-2	Conroy, Raynor, Beckham	8,601
33		18	(h)	Bury	W	5-0	Carmichael 2 Conroy 2, Moyes	9,626
34		21	(a)	Exeter C	W	1-0	Bryson	2,057
35		25	(a)	Lincoln C	D	1-1	Kidd	5,487
36	Apr	1	(h)	Gillingham	D	1-1	Carmichael	9,100
37		8	(a)	Scarborough	D	1-1	Bryson	4,266
38		15	(h)	Wigan A	W	1-0	Smart	10,238
39		17	(a)	Rochdale	W	1-0	Davey	4,012
40		22	(h)	Torquay U	L	0-1		9,173
41		29	(h)	Hartlepool U	W	3-0	Moyes, Holmes, Davey	9,129
42	May	6	(a)	Scunthorpe U	L	1-2	Sale	3,691

FINAL LEAGUE POSITION: 5th in Division Three

Appearances

Sub. Appearances

Goals

Richardson	Fensome	Fleming	Whalley	Hicks	Moyes	Ainsworth	Cartwright	Raynor	Trebble	Bryson	Kidd	Sale	Conroy	Squires	Vaughan	Sharp	Akinson	Holmes	Emerson	Smart	Magee	Rimmer	Lancashire	Davey	Beckham	Carmichael	
1	2	3	4	5	6	7	8	9	10	11																	1
1	2	11	4	5	6	7	8	9*			3	10	12														2
1	2	3	4	5		7	8	12	9†	11	6	14	10*														3
1	2		4		6	7		11		8	3	10	9	5													4
1	2	14	4		6	7	12	9		8*	3	10	11†	5													5
1	2	11†	4	5	6	7*	12	9	14	8	3	10															6
1	2	11	4*	5	6	7	12	9†	14	8	3	10															7
1	2	11	4		6	7	12	9	14	8	3*	10†		5													8
1	2	9	4		6	7		11	10	8	3			5													9
1	2	14	4		6	7	12	11†	10	8*	3	9		5													10
1	2	10	4	5	6	7		11	12	8	3	9*															11
	2	12	4†	5		7	14		10	8	6	9*			1	3	11										12
	2	14	4	5	6	7†		9		8	12	10*			1	3	11										13
	2	7	4†		6		14	9		8	12	10*			1	3	11	5									14
	2	7	12		6		4	9		8		10		5*	1	3	11										15
1	2	12			6	7	4	9		11*	8†		10			3		5					14				16
1	2				6		4	12	7*	11	8	5	10			3				9							17
1	2	12			6		4			11	8	5	10			3				9†	7*		14				18
1	2				6	7				11	8	5	10			3			4	9*			12				19
1	2				6		4			11	8	5	10			3	12			9†	7*		14				20
1°	2				6		4			11	8	5	10†	15		3*	12			9	7		14				21
	2	3			6	7*	4			12	8	5	14		1		11			9†			10				22
	2	3			6		4			11	12	8	5		1		14			9*	7†		10				23
	2	3			6		4			11	12	8	5		1		14			9*	7†		10				24
	2	3			6		4			11	12	8	5		1		14			9*	7†		10				25
	2	12			6	7	4			11	14	8	5		1	3†				9*			10				26
	2				6		4			11	12	8	5		1	3	14			9*	7†		10				27
	2				6	7*	4			11	12	8	5		1	3	10			9							28
	2				6		4			11	8	5	10		1	3	12			9†	7*		14				29
	2				6		4			11	8	5	10		1	3				9*			12	7			30
	2				6		4			11†	8	5	10		1	3				12			9*	7	14		31
	2				6		12	9			8*	5	10		1	3				11				7	4		32
	2				6						8	5	10	5	1	3				11				7	4	9	33
	2				6		12				8	5	10	5	1	3				11*				7	4	9	34
	2				6		12	14			8	5	10	5	1	3				11*				7	4	9†	35
	2				6		12	4			8		10	5	1	3†				11*			14	7		9	36
	2	3			6		4	11			8		10	5	1					12				7		9*	37
	2	3			6†		4	11			8	5	10		1					9*			12	7		14	38
	2	3					4	11			8	5	12	6	1					9†			14	7		10*	39
	2	3					4	11			8	5†	10*	6	1					9			12	7		14	40
	2	3			6		4				8				1			5		11			9	7		10	41
	2*	3			6		12	4			8	5	10†		1					11			9	7		14	42
17	42	20	14		38	16	25	34	8	41	32	10	22	11	25	21	8	5	1	17	14		9	13	4	7	
	7	1			11	4	11			3	3	1			7		1	2	2	8			1		3		
		2	1		4	1	1	3	4	5	3	7	10			1	1			6	1			3	2	3	

1995-96

1	Aug	12	(h)	Lincoln C	L	1-2	Saville	7,813
2		19	(a)	Plymouth Argyle	W	2-0	Hammond (og), Bryson	6,862
3		26	(h)	Wigan A	D	1-1	Atkinson	6,837
4		29	(a)	Bury	D	0-0		4,682
5	Sep	2	(h)	Cambridge U	D	3-3	Saville, Wilkinson, Lancashire	7,034
6		9	(a)	Hereford U	W	1-0	Saville	3,124
7		12	(a)	Colchester U	D	2-2	Cartwright, Bryson	2,869
8		16	(h)	Scunthorpe U	D	2-2	Atkinson, Bryson	7,397
9		23	(a)	Fulham	D	2-2	Bryson (pen), Davey	5,209
10		30	(h)	Chester C	W	2-0	Wilkinson, Saville	8,544
11	Oct	7	(h)	Scarborough	W	3-2	Saville, Wilkinson, Davey	7,702
12		14	(a)	Torquay U	W	4-0	Bryson 2, Saville 2	4,058
13		21	(h)	Mansfield T	W	6-0	Wilkinson 3, Saville 3	8,981
14		28	(a)	Doncaster U	D	2-2	Davey 2	4,413
15		31	(a)	Northampton T	W	2-1	Wilcox, Saville	4,695
16	Nov	4	(h)	Leyton Orient	W	4-0	Saville 3, Davey	9,823
17		18	(a)	Exeter C	D	1-1	Moyes	3,550
18		25	(h)	Hartlepool	W	3-0	Moyes, Atkinson, Saville	9,449
19	Dec	9	(h)	Fulham	D	1-1	Bryson	8,422
20		16	(a)	Chester C	D	1-1	Wilkinson	5,004
21		23	(h)	Gillingham	D	0-0		10,669
22	Jan	1	(h)	Cardiff C	W	5-0	Davey, Brown, Saville 2, Atkinson	8,354
23		6	(a)	Barnet	L	0-1		2,737
24		13	(h)	Plymouth Argyle	W	3-2	Bryson, Davey, Cartwright	11,126
25		20	(a)	Lincoln C	D	0-0		5,185
26		30	(a)	Darlington	W	2-1	Cartwright, Saville	2,599
27	Feb	3	(a)	Wigan A	W	1-0	Kilbane	5,567
28		10	(h)	Barnet	L	0-1		9,974
29		17	(h)	Colchester U	W	2-0	Saville 2	9,335
30		24	(a)	Scunthorpe U	W	2-1	Saville, Lancaster	3,638
31		27	(h)	Hereford U	D	2-2	Atkinson, Saville	9,761
32	Mar	2	(h)	Rochdale	L	1-2	Saville	9,697
33		9	(a)	Gillingham	D	1-1	Davey	10,602
34		12	(a)	Rochdale	W	3-0	Birch, Wilkinson, Moyes	4,597
35		16	(h)	Darlington	D	1-1	Bryson	12,070
36		23	(a)	Cardiff C	W	1-0	Saville	3,511
37		26	(h)	Bury	D	0-0		12,260
38		30	(a)	Scarborough	W	2-1	Davey, Bennett	3,771
39	Apr	2	(h)	Torquay U	W	1-0	Wilkinson	11,965
40		6	(h)	Doncaster R	W	1-0	Birch	12,773
41		8	(a)	Mansfield T	D	0-0		4,661
42		13	(h)	Northampton T	L	0-3		11,774
43		16	(a)	Cambridge U	L	1-2	Saville	2,831
44		20	(a)	Leyton Orient	W	2-0	Saville	5,170
45		27	(a)	Hartlepool U	W	2-0	Davey, Saville	5,076
46	May	4	(h)	Exeter C	W	2-0	Saville, Wilkinson	18,700

FINAL lEAGUE POSITION: 1st in Division Three

Appearances

Sub. Appearances

Goals

Vaughan	Fensome	Fleming	Davey	Kidd	Moyes	Raynor	Bryson	Saville	Wilkinson	Atkinson	Lancashire	Sharp	Magee	Ainsworth	Squires	Holmes	Cartwright	Brown	Richardson	Johnson	Barrick	Smart	Wilcox	Kilbane	McDonald	Bishop	Moilanen	Sparrow	Birch	Grant	Bennet	Gage	Lucas
1	2*	3	4	5	6	7	8	9	10	11	12																						
1	2*	7		5	6		8	9	10	4°		3	11	12	13																		
1	2	3	6				8	9	10	4			11*	12		5	7																
1	2	3	6				8	9	10	4			11			5	7																
1	2	3	6*	13			8	9	10	4	12		11†			5	7°	14															
	2		3			11	8	9	10	4					5		7		1	6													
	2*		3				8	9	10†	4	12				5		7	11†	1	6		13	14										
	2		6				8	9	10		12				1	5	7°	11*	1		3	13											
1	2		7		6		8*	9	10	4						12	11				3	5											
1	2		7		6		8	9	10	4						12	11*				3	5											
1	2		7	12	6		8	9	10	4						13	11°				3	5*											
1	2		7	12	6		8	9	10	4°							11				3	5*	13										
1	2		7*		6		8	9	10	4							11				3	5	12										
1	2		7	12	6		8	9	10	4							11				3	5*											
1	2		7		6		8	9	10	4							11*				3	5	12										
1	2		7		6		8	9	10	4							11				3	5											
1	2		7	12	6		8	9	10	4							11°				3	5*	13										
1	2		7	5	6		8	9	10	4							11				3												
1	2*		7		6		8	9	10	4							11				3	5	12										
1	2		7		6		8	9	10*	4						12	11				3	5											
1	2		7		6		8	9	10	4							11				3	5											
1	2		7	11	6		8	9		4							12				3	5*							10				
1	2*		7°	11	6		8	9		4							12	13			3	5							10				
1			7		6		8	9		4							11				3	5						2	10				
			7		6		8*	9	12	4							11				3	5					1	2	10				
			7	12	6			9	13	4							11				3	5	8*		10°		1	2					
1			7	5*			8°	9	10	4						12	11				3		13					2					
1			7		6			9	12	4*					2		11*				3	5	8						10				
1			7	5	6		8	9	10	4											3							2	11				
1			7	5	6		8	9	10	4							12				3							2	11*				
1			7	5	6*		8	9	10°	4†							11	12			3							2				13	
1			7		6		8	9	12	4										10*	3	5						2°	11†			14	
1			7		6		8	9	10	4											3	5						2	11				
1			7		6		8	9	10	4											3	5	7					2	11				
1			7		6		8	9	10	4											3	5	7*					2	11			12	
1			7	12	6		8	9	10	4											3	5*						2	11				
1			7	5	6		8	9	10	4											3							2	11				
1			7	5	6		8		10	4											3							2	11	9			
1			7	5	6		8		10	4											3							2*	11	9		12	
1			7	5	6		8	9		4											3							2	11		10		
1			7	5	6		8	9	12	4											3							2°	11*		10	13	
1			7	5	6		8	9	12	4°											3							2	11*		10	13	
1			7	12	6		8	9	10	4*											3	5						2	11†			13	
1			7		6		8	9	10	4*											3	5						2	11			12	
			7		6		8	9	10	4											3	5					1	2	11				
1			7	12	6		8	9	10	4°											3	5						2	11*			13	
40	20	5	37	23	41	2	44	44	36	42	2	1	4		3	8	22	6	3	2	39	27	7	8	4	2		13	11		5	4	1
		1		7		1			6	2			4		1	2	4	4			4		1	2	4			3		1	3	3	
			10	3	9		29	10	5								3											2					

61

F.A. CUP

1971/72 SEASON
3rd Round
Jan 15 vs Bristol City (h) 4-2
Att: 13,619 Lynall, Ingram, Clark 2

4th Round
Feb 5 vs Manchester United (h) 0-2
Att: 37,052

1972/73 SEASON
3rd Round
Jan 13 vs Grimsby Town (a) 0-0
Att: 16,000

Replay
Jan 15 vs Grimsby Town (h) 0-1
Att: 13,175

1973/74 SEASON
3rd Round
Jan 5 vs Fulham (a) 0-1
Att: 6,937

1974/75 SEASON
1st Round
Nov 23 vs Blyth Spartans (a) 1-1
Att: 8,500 Holden

Replay
Nov 26 vs Blyth Spartans (h) 5-1
Att: 10,101 Holden 4, Elwiss

2nd Round
Dec 14 vs Bishop Auckland (a) 2-0
Att: 6,500 Charlton, Morley

3rd Round
Jan 4 vs Carlisle United (h) 0-1
Att: 18,682

1975/76 SEASON
1st Round
Nov 22 vs Scunthorpe United (h) 2-1
Att: 8,119 Morley (pen), Elwiss

2nd Round
Dec 13 vs Scarborough (a) 2-3
Att: 4,110 Smith 2

1976/77 SEASON
1st Round
Nov 20 vs Crewe Alexandra (a) 1-1
Att: 6,373 Coleman

Replay
Nov 23 vs Crewe Alexandra (h) 2-2 (aet)
Att: 10,833 D. Davies 2

2nd Replay (at Anfield)
Nov 29 vs Crewe Alexandra 3-0
Att: 7,334 Sadler, Brown, Elwiss

2nd Round
Dec 14 vs Halifax Town (a) 0-1
Att: 5,219

1977/78 SEASON
1st Round
Nov 26 vs Lincoln City (h) 3-2
Att: 6,965 Elwiss 2, Bruce

2nd Round
Dec 17 vs Wrexham (h) 0-2
Att: 11,134

1978/79 SEASON
3rd Round
Jan 16 vs Derby County (h) 3-0
Att: 19,884 Bruce 2, Burns

4th Round
Feb 12 vs Southampton (h) 0-1
Att: 20,727

1979/80 SEASON
3rd Round
Jan 5 vs Ipswich Town (h) 0-3
Att: 16,986

1980/81 SEASON
3rd Round
Jan 3 vs Bristol Rovers (h) 3-4
Att: 6,248 Houston, Bruce, McGee

1981/82 SEASON
1st Round
Nov 21 vs Chesterfield (a) 1-4
Att: 5,435 Doyle

1982/83 SEASON
1st Round
Nov 20 vs Shepshed Charterhouse (h) 5-1
Att: 6,200 Elliott 2, Kelly, Coleman, McAteer

2nd Round
Dec 11 vs Blackpool (h) 2-1
Att: 14,008 Coleman, O'Riordan

3rd Round
Jan 8 vs Leeds United (a) 0-3
Att: 16,816

1983/84 SEASON
1st Round
Nov 19 vs Scunthorpe United (a) 0-1
Att: 3,484

1984/85 SEASON
1st Round
Nov 17 vs Bury (h) 4-3
Att: 5,013 Gray, Johnson 2, Naughton

2nd Round
Dec 8 vs Telford United (h) 1-4
Att: 6,134 Hunter

1985/86 SEASON
1st Round
Nov 16 vs Walsall (a) 3-7
Att: 4,035 Thomas, Brazil, Martin

1986/87 SEASON
1st Round
Nov 15 vs Bury (h) 5-1
Att: 7,949 Thomas 3 (1 pen), Jones, Williams

2nd Round (at Blackburn)
Dec 6 vs Chorley (a) 0-0
Att: 15,153

Replay
Dec 9 vs Chorley (h) 5-0
Att: 16,417 Thomas 3 (1 pen), Williams, Brazil

3rd Round
Jan 10 vs Middlesbrough (a) 1-0
Att: 15,458 Hildersley

4th Round
Jan 31 vs Newcastle United (a) 0-2
Att: 30,495

1987/88 SEASON
1st Round
Nov 14 vs Mansfield Town (h) 1-1
Att: 7,415 Atkins

Replay
Nov 17 vs Mansfield Town (a) 2-4
Att: 4,682 Brazil, Jemson

1988/89 SEASON
1st Round
Nov 19 vs Tranmere Rovers (h) 1-1
Att: 7,734 Atkins

Replay
Nov 22 vs Tranmere Rovers (a) 0-3
Att: 7,676

1989/90 SEASON
1st Round
Nov 18 vs Tranmere Rovers (h) 1-0
Att: 7,521 Joyce

2nd Round
Dec 9 vs Whitley Bay (a) 0-2
Att: 4,500

1990/91 SEASON
1st Round
Nov 17 vs Mansfield Town (h) 0-1
Att: 5,230

1991/92 SEASON
1st Round
Nov 16 vs Mansfield Town (a) 1-1 (match abandoned after 32 minutes due to fog)
Att: – Shaw

Replay
Nov 27 vs Mansfield Town (a) 1-0
Att: 7,509 Thomas

2nd Round
Dec 7 vs Witton Albion (h) 5-1
Att: 6,736 Shaw, Swann, Senior, Flynn, Greenwood

3rd Round
Jan 4 vs Sheffield Wednesday (h) 0-2
Att: 14,337

1992/93 SEASON
1st Round
Nov 14 vs Bradford City (a) 1-1
Att: 8,553 Fowler

Replay
Nov 25 vs Bradford City (h) 4-5
Att: 7,905 Graham, Ellis, Davidson, Callaghan

1993/94 SEASON
1st Round
Nov 13 vs Mansfield Town (a) 2-1
Att: 4,119 Ellis 2 (1 pen)

2nd Round
Dec 4 vs Shrewsbury Town (a) 1-0
Att: 5,018 Raynor

3rd Round
Jan 8 vs Bournemouth (h) 2-1
Att: 8,457 Moyes, Conroy

4th Round
Jan 29 vs Kidderminster (a) 0-1
Att: 7,000

1994/95 SEASON
1st Round
Nov 14 vs Blackpool (h) 1-0
Att: 14,036 Conroy

2nd Round
Dec 3 vs Walsall (h) 1-1
Att: 9,767 Smart

Replay
Dec 13 vs Walsall (a) 0-4
Att: 6,468

1995/96 SEASON
1st Round
Nov 11 vs Carlisle United (a) 2-1
Att: 7,046 Cartwright, Wilcox

2nd Round
Dec 2 vs Bradford City (a) 1-2
Att: 7,602 Wilkinson

LEAGUE CUP

1971/72 SEASON
1st Round
Aug 18 vs Barrow (a) 2-0
Att: 4,319 Clarke (og), Ham

2nd Round
Sep 8 vs Tranmere Rovers (a) 1-0
Att: 5,873 McIlmoyle

3rd Round
Oct 6 vs Watford (a) 1-1
Att: 8,853 Spavin

Replay
Oct 11 vs Watford (h) 2-1
Att: 12,436 Spavin, McIlmoyle

4th Round
Oct 27 vs Tottenham Hotspur (a) 1-1
Att: 30,338 Lyall

Replay
Nov 8 vs Tottenham Hotspur (h) 1-2
Att: 28,000 McIlmoyle

1972/73 SEASON
1st Round
Aug 16 vs Workington Town (a) 0-1
Att: 4,055

1973/74 SEASON
1st Round
Sep 3 vs Bolton Wanderers (h) 0-2
Att: 18,571

1974/75 SEASON
1st Round
Aug 20 vs Rochdale (h) 1-0
Att: 7,780 Holden

2nd Round
Sep 10 vs Sunderland (h) 2-0
Att: 13,279 Morley, Charlton

3rd Round
Oct 9 vs Chester City (a) 0-1
Att: 11,262

1975/76 SEASON
1st Round (1st leg)
Aug 19 vs Blackburn Rovers (h) 2-0
Att: 11,503 Morley, Treacy

1st Round (2nd leg)
Aug 27 vs Blackburn Rvrs. (a) 0-0 (agg 2-0)
Att: 14,077

2nd Round
Sep 9 vs Hull City (a) 2-4
Att: 5,095 Morley, Treacy

1976/77 SEASON
1st Round (1st leg)
Aug 14 vs Bury (a) 1-2
Att: 5,858 Brown

1st Round (2nd leg)
Aug 17 vs Bury (h) 1-1 (aggregate 2-3)
Att: 7,521 Smith

1977/78 SEASON
1st Round (1st leg)
Aug 13 vs Port Vale (a) 1-2
Att: 4,530 Bruce

1st Round (2nd leg)
Aug 16 vs Port Vale (h) 2-1 (agg 3-3)
Att: 5,816 Elwiss 2

Replay
Aug 23 vs Port Vale (h) 2-1
Att: 2,201 Elwiss, McGifford (og)

2nd Round
Aug 30 vs Walsall (a) 0-0
Att: 5,445

Replay
Sep 6 vs Walsall (h) 0-1
Att: 7,079

1978/79 SEASON
1st Round (1st leg)
Aug 12 vs Huddersfield Town (h) 3-0
Att: 6,841 Baxter, Bruce 2

1st Round (2nd leg)
Aug 15 vs Huddersfield T. (a) 2-2 (agg. 5-2)
Att: 3,435 Bruce, Thomas

2nd Round
Aug 29 vs Queen's Park Rangers (h) 1-3
Att: 14,913 Fisher

1979/80 SEASON
2nd Round (1st leg)
Aug 28 vs Birmingham City (a) 1-2
Att: 13,660 Potts

2nd Round (2nd leg)
Sep 4 vs Birmingham City (h) 0-1 (agg. 1-3)
Att: 11,043

1980/81 SEASON
2nd Round (1st leg)
Aug 26 vs Wigan Athletic (h) 1-0
Att: 8,073 McGee

2nd Round (2nd leg)
Sep 3 vs Wigan Athletic (a) 2-1 (agg. 3-1)
Att: 9,692 McGee, Coleman

3rd Round
Sep 23 vs Oxford United (h) 1-0
Att: 5,722 Coleman

4th Round
Oct 29 vs West Bromwich Albion (a) 0-0
Att: 17,579

Replay
Nov 4 vs West Bromwich Albion (h) 1-1
Att: 14,420 Bell

2nd Replay
Nov 12 vs West Bromwich Albion (a) 1-2
Att: 15,218 Bruce

1981/82 SEASON
1st Round (1st leg)
Sep 1 vs Halifax Town (a) 2-1
Att: 2,719 Clark, Naughton

1st Round (2nd leg)
Sep 15 vs Halifax Town (h) 0-0 (agg. 2-1)
Att: 4,090

2nd Round (1st leg)
Oct 6 vs Leicester City (h) 1-0
Att: 5,382 Bruce

2nd Round (2nd leg)
Oct 28 vs Leicester City (a) 0-4 (agg. 1-4)
Att: 7,685

1982/83 SEASON
1st Round (1st leg)
Aug 31 vs Walsall (a) 1-0
Att: 2,490 Naughton

1st Round (2nd leg)
Sep 14 vs Walsall (h) 1-1
Att: 3,137 Elliott

2nd Round (1st leg)
Oct 6 vs Norwich City (a) 1-2
Att: 7,273 Bruce

2nd Round (2nd leg)
Oct 26 vs Norwich City (h) 1-2 (agg. 2-4)
Att: 6,082 Elliott

1983/84 SEASON
1st Round (1st leg)
Aug 30 vs Tranmere Rovers (h) 0-1
Att: 3,231 Kelly

1st Round (2nd leg)
Sep 12 vs Tranmere Rovers (a) 0-0 (agg 0-1)
Att: 2,986

1984/85 SEASON
1st Round (1st leg)
Aug 28 vs Tranmere Rovers (a) 3-2
Att: 2,015 Kelly, Farrelly, Twentyman

1st Round (2nd leg)
Sep 4 vs Tranmere R. (h) 2-2 (aet) (agg 5-4)
Att: 2,557 Houghton, Wilkins

2nd Round (1st leg)
Sep 25 vs Norwich City (h) 3-3
Att: 5,265 Houghton, Wilkins, Twentyman

2nd Round (2nd leg)
Oct 10 vs Norwich City (a) 1-6 (aggreg. 4-9)
Att: 13,506 Twentyman

1985/86 SEASON
1st Round (1st leg)
Aug 20 vs Blackpool (h) 2-1
Att: 4,704 Keen, Foster

1st Round (2nd leg)
Sep 3 vs Blackpool (a) 3-1 (aggregate 5-2)
Att: 5,043 Rudge, Twentyman, Brazil

2nd Round (1st leg)
Sep 30 vs Norwich City (h) 1-1
Att: 4,330 Brazil (pen)

2nd Round (2nd leg)
Oct 7 vs Norwich City (a) 1-2 (aggreg. 2-3)
Att: 11,537 Brazil

1986/87 SEASON
1st Round (1st leg)
Aug 29 vs Blackpool (a) 0-0
Att: 3,929

1st Round (2nd leg)
Sep 2 vs BLackpool (h) 2-1 (aggregate 2-1)
Att: 5,914 Hildersley, Williams

2nd Round (1st leg)
Sep 23 vs West Ham United (h) 1-1
Att: 13,153 Allardyce

2nd Round (2nd leg)
Oct 7 vs West Ham United (a) 1-4 (agg 2-6)
Att: 12,742 Williams

1987/88 SEASON
1st Round (1st leg)
Aug 18 vs Bury (a) 2-2
Att: 2,363 Allardyce, Brazil

1st Round (2nd leg)
Aug 25 vs Bury (h) 2-3
Att: 4,923 Brazil, Hill (og)

1988/89 SEASON
1st Round (1st leg)
Aug 29 vs Wigan Athletic (a) 0-0
Att: 4,035

1st Round (2nd leg)
Sep 5 vs Wigan Athletic (h) 1-0 (agg. 1-0)
Att: 4,945 Brazil

2nd Round (1st leg)
Sep 28 vs Norwich City (a) 0-2
Att: 7,484

2nd Round (2nd leg)
Oct 11 vs Norwich City (h) 0-3 (agg. 0-5)
Att: 7,002

1989/90 SEASON
1st Round (1st leg)
Aug 22 vs Tranmere Rovers (h) 3-4
Att: 4,632 Shaw 3 (1 pen)

1st Round (2nd leg)
Aug 29 vs Tranmere Rovers (a) 1-3 (agg 4-7)
Att: 5,275 Shaw

1990/91 SEASON
1st Round (1st leg)
Aug 28 vs Chester City (h) 2-0
Att: 3,503 Shaw, Swann

1st Round (2nd leg)
Sep 4 vs Chester City (a) 1-5 (aet) (agg 3-5)
Att: 1,009 Swann

1991/92 SEASON
1st Round (1st leg)
Aug 20 vs Scarborough (h) 5-4
Att: 2,683 Wrightson, Swann 2, Shaw, Joyce
(pen)

1st Round (2nd leg)
Aug 28 vs Scarborough (a) 1-3 (agg. 6-7)
Att: 2,035 Joyce

1992/93 SEASON
1st Round (1st leg)
Aug 18 vs Stoke City (h) 2-1
Att: 5,581 Tinkler, Ellis

1st Round (2nd leg)
Aug 26 vs Stoke City (a) 0-4 (aggreg. 2-5)
Att: 9,745

1993/94 SEASON
1st Round (1st leg)
Aug 17 vs Burnley (h) 1-2
Att: 6,283 Ellis

1st Round (2nd leg)
Aug 25 vs Burnley (a) 1-4 (aggregate 2-6)
Att: 9,346 Cartwright

1994/95 SEASON
1st Round (1st leg)
Aug 17 vs Stockport County (h) 1-1
Att: 2,385 Fensome (pen)

1st Round (2nd leg)
Aug 23 vs Stockport Co. (a) 1-4 (agg. 2-5)
Att: 5,450 Mayes

1995/96 SEASON
1st Round (1st leg)
Aug 14 vs Sunderland (h) 1-1
Att: 6,323 Kidd

1st Round (2nd leg)
Aug 23 vs Sunderland (a) 2-3 (aggreg. 3-4)
Att: 7,407 Cartwright, Bryson

1971-72 SEASON

SECOND DIVISION

Norwich City	42	21	15	6	60	36	57
Birmingham City	42	19	18	5	60	31	56
Millwall	42	19	17	6	64	46	55
Q.P.R.	42	20	14	8	57	28	54
Sunderland	42	17	16	9	67	57	50
Blackpool	42	20	7	15	70	50	47
Burnley	42	20	6	16	70	55	46
Bristol City	42	18	10	14	61	49	46
Middlesbrough	42	19	8	15	50	48	46
Carlisle United	42	17	9	16	61	57	43
Swindon Town	42	15	12	15	47	47	42
Hull City	42	14	10	18	49	53	38
Luton Town	42	10	18	14	43	48	38
Sheffield Wednesday	42	13	12	17	51	58	38
Oxford United	42	12	14	16	43	55	38
Portsmouth	42	12	13	17	59	68	37
Orient	42	14	9	19	50	61	37
Preston North End	**42**	**12**	**12**	**18**	**52**	**58**	**36**
Cardiff City	42	10	14	18	56	69	34
Fulham	42	12	10	20	45	68	34
Charlton Athletic	42	12	9	21	55	77	33
Watford	42	5	9	28	24	75	19

1973-74 SEASON

SECOND DIVISION

Middlesbrough	42	27	11	4	77	30	65
Luton Town	42	19	12	11	64	51	50
Carlisle United	42	20	9	13	61	48	49
Orient	42	15	18	9	55	42	48
Blackpool	42	17	13	12	57	40	47
Sunderland	42	19	9	14	58	44	47
Nottingham Forest	42	15	15	12	57	43	45
West Brom. Albion	42	14	16	12	48	45	44
Hull City	42	13	17	12	46	47	43
Notts County	42	15	13	14	55	60	43
Bolton Wanderers	42	15	12	15	44	40	42
Millwall	42	14	14	14	51	51	42
Fulham	42	16	10	16	39	43	42
Aston Villa	42	13	15	14	48	45	41
Portsmouth	42	14	12	16	45	62	40
Bristol City	42	14	10	18	47	54	38
Cardiff City	42	10	16	16	49	62	36
Oxford United	42	10	16	16	35	46	36
Sheffield Wednesday	42	12	11	19	51	63	35
Crystal Palace	42	11	12	19	43	56	34
Preston North End *	**42**	**9**	**14**	**19**	**40**	**62**	**31**
Swindon Town	42	7	11	24	36	72	25

* Preston - one point deducted for fielding ineligible player

1975-76 SEASON

THIRD DIVISION

Hereford United	46	26	11	9	86	55	63
Cardiff City	46	22	13	11	69	48	57
Millwall	46	20	16	10	54	43	56
Brighton & Hove Alb.	46	22	9	15	78	53	53
Crystal Palace	46	18	17	11	61	46	53
Wrexham	46	20	12	14	66	55	52
Walsall	46	18	14	14	74	61	50
Preston North End	**46**	**19**	**10**	**17**	**62**	**57**	**48**
Shrewsbury Town	46	19	10	17	61	59	48
Peterborough United	46	15	18	13	63	63	48
Mansfield Town	46	16	15	15	58	52	47

1972-73 SEASON

SECOND DIVISION

Burnley	42	24	14	4	72	35	62
Q.P.R.	42	24	13	5	81	37	61
Aston Villa	42	18	14	10	51	47	50
Middlesbrough	42	17	13	12	46	43	47
Bristol City	42	17	12	13	63	51	46
Sunderland	42	17	12	13	59	49	46
Blackpool	42	18	10	14	56	51	46
Oxford United	42	19	7	16	52	43	45
Fulham	42	16	12	14	58	49	44
Sheffield Wednesday	42	17	10	15	59	55	44
Millwall	42	16	10	16	55	47	42
Luton Town	42	15	11	16	44	43	41
Hull City	42	14	12	16	64	49	40
Nottingham Forest	42	14	12	16	47	52	40
Orient	42	12	12	18	49	53	36
Swindon Town	42	10	16	16	46	60	36
Portsmouth	42	12	11	19	42	59	35
Carlisle United	42	11	12	19	50	52	34
Preston North End	**42**	**11**	**12**	**19**	**37**	**64**	**34**
Cardiff City	42	11	11	20	43	58	33
Huddersfield Town	42	8	17	17	36	56	33
Brighton & Hove Alb.	42	8	13	21	46	83	29

1974-75 SEASON

THIRD DIVISION

Blackburn Rovers	46	22	16	8	68	45	60
Plymouth Argyle	46	24	11	11	79	58	59
Charlton Athletic	46	22	11	13	76	61	55
Swindon Town	46	21	11	14	64	58	53
Crystal Palace	46	18	15	13	66	57	51
Port Vale	46	18	15	13	61	54	51
Peterborough United	46	19	12	15	47	53	50
Walsall	46	18	13	15	67	52	49
Preston North End	**46**	**19**	**11**	**16**	**63**	**56**	**49**
Gillingham	46	17	14	15	65	60	48
Colchester United	46	17	13	16	70	63	47
Hereford Town	46	16	14	16	64	66	46
Wrexham	46	15	15	16	65	55	45
Bury	46	16	12	18	53	50	44
Chesterfield	46	16	12	18	62	66	44
Grimsby Town	46	15	13	18	55	64	43
Halifax Town	46	13	17	16	49	65	43
Southend United	46	13	16	17	46	51	42
Brighton & Hove Alb.	46	16	10	20	56	64	42
* Aldershot	46	14	11	21	53	63	38
Bournemouth	46	13	12	21	44	58	38
Tranmere Rovers	46	14	9	23	55	57	37
Watford	46	10	17	19	52	75	37
Huddersfield Town	46	11	10	25	47	76	32

* One point deducted for using unregistered player

Port Vale	46	15	16	15	55	54	46
Bury	46	14	16	16	51	46	44
Chesterfield	46	17	9	20	69	69	43
Gillingham	46	12	19	15	58	68	43
Rotherham United	46	15	12	19	54	65	42
Chester City	46	15	12	19	53	62	42
Grimsby Town	46	15	10	21	62	74	40
Swindon Town	46	16	8	22	62	75	40
Sheffield Wednesday	46	12	16	18	48	59	40
Aldershot	46	13	13	20	59	75	39
Colchester United	46	12	14	20	41	65	38
Southend United	46	12	13	21	65	75	37
Halifax Town	46	11	13	22	41	61	35

1976-77 SEASON

THIRD DIVISION

Mansfield Town	46	28	8	10	78	33	64
Brighton & Hove Alb.	46	25	11	10	83	39	61
Crystal Palace	46	23	13	10	68	40	59
Rotherham United	46	22	15	9	69	44	59
Wrexham	46	24	10	12	80	54	58
Preston North End	**46**	**21**	**12**	**13**	**64**	**43**	**54**
Bury	46	23	8	15	64	59	54
Sheffield Wednesday	46	22	9	15	65	55	53
Lincoln City	46	25	14	13	77	70	52
Shrewsbury Town	46	18	11	17	65	59	47
Swindon Town	46	15	15	16	68	75	45
Gillingham	46	14	12	18	55	64	44
Chester City	46	18	8	20	48	58	44
Tranmere Rovers	46	13	17	16	51	53	43
Walsall	46	13	15	18	57	65	41
Peterborough United	46	13	15	18	55	65	41
Oxford United	46	12	15	19	55	65	39
Chesterfield	46	14	10	22	56	64	38
Port Vale	46	11	16	19	47	71	38
Portsmouth	46	11	14	21	43	70	35
Reading	46	13	9	24	49	73	35
Northampton Town	46	13	8	25	60	75	34
Grimsby Town	46	12	9	25	45	69	33
York City	46	10	12	24	50	89	32

1977-78 SEASON

THIRD DIVISION

Wrexham	46	23	15	8	78	45	61
Cambridge United	46	23	12	11	72	51	58
Preston North End	**46**	**20**	**16**	**10**	**63**	**38**	**56**
Peterborough United	46	20	16	10	47	33	56
Chester City	46	16	22	8	59	56	54
Walsall	46	18	17	11	61	50	53
Gillingham	46	15	20	11	67	60	50
Colchester United	46	15	18	13	55	44	48
Chesterfield	46	17	14	15	58	49	48
Swindon Town	46	16	16	14	67	60	48
Shrewsbury Town	46	16	15	15	63	57	47
Tranmere Rovers	46	16	15	15	57	52	47
Carlisle United	46	14	19	13	59	59	47
Sheffield Wednesday	46	15	16	15	50	52	46
Bury	46	13	19	14	62	56	45
Lincoln City	46	15	15	16	53	61	45
Exeter City	46	15	14	17	49	59	44
Oxford United	46	13	14	19	64	67	40
Plymouth Argyle	46	11	17	18	61	68	39
Rotherham United	46	13	13	20	51	68	39
Port Vale	46	8	20	18	46	67	36
Bradford City	46	12	10	24	56	86	34
Hereford United	46	9	14	23	34	60	32
Portsmouth	46	7	17	22	31	75	31

1978-79 SEASON

SECOND DIVISION

Crystal Palace	42	19	19	4	51	24	57
Brighton & Hove Alb.	42	23	10	9	72	39	56
Stoke City	42	20	16	6	58	31	56
Sunderland	42	22	11	9	70	44	55
West Ham United	42	18	14	10	70	39	50
Notts County	42	14	16	12	48	60	44
Preston North End	**42**	**12**	**18**	**12**	**59**	**57**	**42**
Newcastle United	42	17	8	17	51	55	42
Cardiff City	42	16	10	16	56	70	42
Fulham	42	13	15	14	50	47	41
Orient	42	15	10	17	51	51	40
Cambridge United	42	12	16	14	44	52	40
Burnley	42	14	12	16	51	62	40
Oldham Athletic	42	13	13	16	52	61	39
Wrexham	42	12	14	16	45	42	38
Bristol Rovers	42	14	10	18	48	60	38
Leicester City	42	10	17	15	43	52	37
Luton Town	42	13	10	19	60	57	36
Charlton Athletic	42	11	13	18	60	69	35
Sheffield United	42	11	12	19	52	69	34
Millwall	42	11	10	21	42	61	32
Blackburn Rovers	42	10	10	22	41	72	30

1979-80 SEASON

SECOND DIVISION

Leicester City	42	21	13	8	58	38	55
Sunderland	42	21	12	9	69	42	54
Birmingham City	42	21	11	10	58	38	53
Chelsea	42	23	7	12	66	52	53
Q.P.R.	42	18	13	11	75	53	49
Luton Town	42	16	17	9	66	45	49
West Ham United	42	20	7	15	54	43	47
Cambridge United	42	14	16	12	61	53	44
Newcastle United	42	15	14	13	53	49	44
Preston North End	**42**	**12**	**19**	**11**	**56**	**52**	**43**
Oldham Athletic	42	16	11	15	49	53	43
Swansea City	42	17	9	16	48	53	43
Shrewsbury Town	42	18	5	19	60	53	41
Orient	42	12	17	13	48	54	41
Cardiff City	42	16	8	18	41	48	40
Wrexham	42	16	6	20	40	49	38
Notts County	42	11	15	16	51	52	37
Watford	42	12	13	17	39	46	37
Bristol Rovers	42	11	13	18	50	64	35
Fulham	42	11	7	24	42	74	29
Burnley	42	6	15	21	39	73	27
Charlton Athletic	42	6	10	26	39	78	22

1980-81 SEASON

SECOND DIVISION

West Ham United	42	28	10	4	79	29	66
Notts County	42	18	17	7	49	38	53
Swansea City	42	18	14	10	64	44	50
Blackburn Rovers	42	16	18	8	42	29	50
Luton Town	42	18	12	12	61	46	48
Derby County	42	15	15	12	57	52	45
Grimsby Town	42	15	15	12	44	42	45
QPR	42	15	13	14	56	46	43
Watford	42	16	11	15	50	45	43
Sheffield Wednesday	42	17	8	17	53	51	42
Newcastle United	42	14	14	14	30	45	42
Chelsea	42	14	12	16	46	41	40
Cambridge United	42	17	6	17	53	65	40
Shrewsbury Town	42	11	17	14	46	47	39
Oldham Athletic	42	12	15	15	39	48	39
Wrexham	42	12	14	16	43	45	38
Orient	42	13	12	17	52	56	38
Bolton Wanderers	42	14	10	18	61	66	38
Cardiff City	42	12	12	18	44	60	36
Preston North End	**42**	**11**	**14**	**17**	**41**	**62**	**36**
Bristol City	42	7	16	19	29	51	30
Bristol Rovers	42	5	13	24	34	65	23

1981-82 SEASON

THIRD DIVISION

	P	W	D	L	F	A	Pts
Burnley	46	21	17	8	66	49	80
Carlisle United	46	23	11	12	65	50	80
Fulham	46	21	15	10	77	51	78
Lincoln City	46	21	14	11	66	40	77
Oxford United	46	19	14	13	63	49	71
Gillingham	46	20	11	15	64	56	71
Southend United	46	18	15	13	63	51	69
Brentford	46	19	11	16	56	47	68
Millwall	46	18	13	15	62	62	67
Plymouth Argyle	46	18	11	17	64	56	65
Chesterfield	46	18	10	18	67	58	64
Reading	46	17	11	18	67	75	62
Portsmouth	46	14	19	13	56	51	61
Preston North End	**46**	**16**	**13**	**17**	**50**	**56**	**61**
Bristol Rovers *	46	18	9	19	58	65	61
Newport County	46	14	16	16	54	54	58
Huddersfield Town	46	15	12	19	64	59	57
Exeter City	46	16	9	21	71	84	57
Doncaster Rovers	46	13	17	16	55	68	56
Walsall	46	13	14	19	51	55	53
Wimbledon	46	14	11	21	61	75	53
Swindon Town	46	13	13	20	55	71	52
Bristol City	46	11	13	22	40	65	46
Chester City	46	7	11	28	36	78	32

* 2 points deducted by the League

1982-83 SEASON

THIRD DIVISION

	P	W	D	L	F	A	Pts
Portsmouth	46	27	10	9	74	41	91
Cardiff City	46	25	11	10	76	50	86
Huddersfield Town	46	23	13	10	84	49	82
Newport County	46	23	9	14	76	54	78
Oxford United	46	22	12	12	71	53	78
Lincoln City	46	23	7	16	77	51	76
Bristol Rovers	46	22	9	15	84	57	75
Plymouth Argyle	46	19	8	19	61	66	65
Brentford	46	18	10	18	88	77	64
Walsall	46	17	13	16	64	63	64
Sheffield United	46	19	7	20	62	64	64
Bradford City	46	16	13	17	68	69	61
Gillingham	46	16	13	17	58	59	61
Bournemouth	46	16	13	17	59	68	61
Southend United	46	15	14	17	66	65	59
Preston North End	**46**	**15**	**13**	**18**	**60**	**69**	**58**
Millwall	46	14	13	19	64	78	55
Wigan	46	15	9	22	60	72	54
Exeter City	46	14	12	20	81	104	54
Orient	46	15	9	22	64	88	54
Reading	46	12	17	17	63	80	53
Wrexham	46	12	15	19	57	76	51
Doncaster Rovers	46	9	11	26	57	97	38
Chesterfield	46	8	13	25	44	68	37

1983-84 SEASON

THIRD DIVISION

	P	W	D	L	F	A	Pts
Oxford United	46	28	11	7	91	50	95
Wimbledon	46	26	9	11	97	76	87
Sheffield United	46	24	11	11	86	53	83
Hull City	46	23	14	9	71	38	83
Bristol Rovers	46	22	13	11	68	54	79
Walsall	46	22	9	15	68	61	75
Bradford City	46	20	11	15	73	65	71
Gillingham	46	20	10	16	74	69	70
Millwall	46	18	13	15	71	65	67
Bolton Wanderers	46	18	10	18	56	60	64
Orient	46	18	9	19	71	81	63
Burnley	46	16	14	16	76	61	62
Newport County	46	16	14	16	58	75	62
Lincoln City	46	17	10	19	59	62	61
Wigan Athletic	46	16	13	17	46	56	61
Preston North End	**46**	**15**	**11**	**20**	**66**	**66**	**56**
Bournemouth	46	16	7	23	63	73	55
Rotherham United	46	15	9	22	57	64	54
Plymouth Argyle	46	13	12	21	56	62	51
Brentford	46	11	16	19	69	79	49
Scunthorpe United	46	9	19	18	54	73	46
Southend United	46	10	14	22	55	76	44
Port Vale	46	11	10	25	51	83	43
Exeter City	46	6	15	25	50	84	33

1984-85 SEASON

THIRD DIVISION

	P	W	D	L	F	A	Pts
Bradford City	46	28	10	8	77	45	94
Millwall	46	26	12	8	83	42	90
Hull City	46	25	12	9	88	49	87
Gillingham	46	25	8	13	80	62	83
Bristol City	46	24	9	13	74	47	81
Bristol Rovers	46	21	12	13	66	48	75
Derby County	46	19	13	14	65	54	70
York City	46	20	9	17	70	57	69
Reading	46	19	12	15	68	62	69
Bournemouth	46	19	11	16	57	46	68
Walsall	46	18	13	15	58	52	67
Rotherham United	46	18	11	17	55	55	65
Brentford	46	16	14	16	62	64	62
Doncaster Rovers	46	17	8	21	72	74	59
Plymouth Argyle	46	15	14	17	62	65	59
Wigan Athletic	46	15	14	17	60	64	59
Bolton Wanderers	46	16	6	24	69	75	54
Newport County	46	13	13	20	55	67	52
Lincoln City	46	11	18	17	50	51	51
Swansea City	46	12	11	23	53	80	47
Burnley	46	11	13	22	60	73	46
Orient	46	11	13	22	51	76	46
Preston North End	**46**	**13**	**7**	**26**	**51**	**100**	**46**
Cambridge United	46	4	9	33	37	95	21

1985-86 SEASON

FOURTH DIVISION

	P	W	D	L	F	A	Pts
Swindon Town	46	32	6	8	82	43	102
Chester City	46	23	15	8	83	50	84
Mansfield Town	46	23	12	11	74	47	81
Port Vale	46	21	16	9	67	37	79
Orient	46	20	12	14	79	64	72
Colchester United	46	19	13	14	88	63	70
Hartlepool	46	20	10	16	68	67	70
Northampton Town	46	18	10	18	79	58	64
Southend United	46	18	10	18	69	67	64
Hereford United	46	18	10	18	74	73	64
Stockport County	46	17	13	16	63	71	64
Crewe Alexandra	46	18	9	19	54	61	63
Wrexham	46	17	9	20	68	80	60
Burnley	46	16	11	19	60	65	59
Scunthorpe United	46	15	14	19	50	55	59
Aldershot	46	17	7	22	66	74	58
Peterborough United	46	13	17	16	52	64	56
Rochdale	46	14	13	19	57	77	55
Tranmere Rovers	46	15	9	22	74	73	54
Halifax Town	46	14	12	20	60	71	54
Exeter City	46	13	15	18	47	59	54
Cambridge United	46	15	9	22	65	80	54
Preston North End	**46**	**11**	**10**	**25**	**54**	**89**	**43**
Torquay United	46	9	10	27	43	88	37

1986-87 SEASON

FOURTH DIVISION

Northampton Town	46	30	9	7	103	53	99
Preston North End	**46**	**26**	**12**	**8**	**72**	**47**	**90**
Southend United	46	25	5	16	68	55	80
Wolves	46	24	7	15	69	50	79
Colchester United	46	21	7	18	64	56	70
Aldershot	46	20	10	16	64	57	70
Orient	46	20	9	17	64	61	69
Scunthorpe United	46	18	12	16	73	57	66
Wrexham	46	15	20	11	70	51	65
Peterborough United	46	17	14	15	57	50	65
Cambridge United	46	17	11	18	60	62	62
Swansea City	46	17	11	18	56	61	62
Cardiff City	46	15	16	15	48	50	61
Exeter City	46	11	23	12	53	49	56
Halifax City	46	15	10	21	59	74	55
Hereford United	46	14	11	21	60	61	53
Crewe Alexandra	46	13	14	19	70	72	53
Hartlepool United	46	11	18	17	44	65	51
Stockport County	46	13	12	21	40	69	51
Tranmere Rovers	46	11	17	18	54	72	50
Rochdale	46	11	17	18	54	73	50
Burnley	46	12	13	21	53	74	49
Torquay United	46	10	18	18	56	72	48
Lincoln City	46	12	12	22	45	65	48

1987-88 SEASON

THIRD DIVISION

Sunderland	46	27	12	7	92	48	93
Brighton & Hove Alb.	46	23	15	8	69	47	84
Walsall	46	23	13	10	68	50	82
Notts County	46	23	12	11	82	49	81
Bristol City	46	21	12	13	77	62	75
Northampton Town	46	18	19	9	70	51	73
Wigan Athletic	46	20	12	14	70	61	72
Bristol Rovers	46	18	12	16	68	56	66
Fulham	46	19	9	18	69	60	66
Blackpool	46	17	14	15	71	62	65
Port Vale	46	18	11	17	58	56	65
Brentford	46	16	14	16	53	59	62
Gillingham	46	14	17	15	77	61	59
Bury	46	15	14	17	58	57	59
Chester City	46	14	16	16	51	62	58
Preston North End	**46**	**15**	**13**	**18**	**48**	**59**	**58**
Southend United	46	14	13	19	65	83	55
Chesterfield	46	15	10	21	41	70	55
Mansfield Town	46	14	12	20	48	59	54
Aldershot	46	15	8	23	64	74	53
Rotherham United	46	12	16	18	50	66	52
Grimsby Town	46	12	14	20	48	58	50
York City	46	8	9	29	48	91	33
Doncaster Rovers	46	8	9	29	40	84	33

1988-89 SEASON

THIRD DIVISION

Wolves	46	26	14	6	96	49	92
Sheffield United	46	25	9	12	93	54	84
Port Vale	46	24	12	10	78	48	84
Fulham	46	22	9	15	69	67	75
Bristol Rovers	46	19	17	10	67	51	74
Preston North End	**46**	**19**	**15**	**12**	**79**	**60**	**72**
Brentford	46	18	14	14	66	61	68
Chester City	46	19	11	16	64	61	68
Notts County	46	18	13	15	64	54	67
Bolton Wanderers	46	16	16	14	58	54	64
Bristol City	46	18	9	19	53	55	63
Swansea City	46	15	16	15	51	53	61
Bury	46	16	13	17	55	67	61
Huddersfield Town	46	17	9	20	63	73	60
Mansfield Town	46	14	17	15	48	52	59
Cardiff City	46	14	15	17	44	56	57
Wigan Athletic	46	14	14	18	55	53	56
Reading	46	15	11	20	68	72	56
Blackpool	46	14	13	19	56	59	54
Northampton Town	46	16	6	24	66	76	54
Southend United	46	13	15	18	56	75	54
Chesterfield	46	14	7	25	51	86	49
Gillingham	46	12	4	30	47	81	40
Aldershot	46	8	13	25	48	78	37

1989-90 SEASON

THIRD DIVISION

Bristol Rovers	46	26	15	5	71	35	93
Bristol City	46	27	10	9	76	40	91
Notts County	46	25	12	9	73	53	87
Tranmere Rovers	46	23	11	12	86	49	80
Bury	46	21	11	14	70	49	74
Bolton Wanderers	46	18	15	13	59	48	69
Birmingham City	46	18	12	16	60	59	66
Huddersfield Town	46	17	14	15	61	62	65
Rotherham United	46	17	13	16	71	62	64
Reading	46	15	19	12	57	53	64
Shrewsbury Town	46	16	15	15	59	54	63
Crewe Alexandra	46	15	17	14	56	53	62
Brentford	46	18	7	21	66	66	61
Leyton Orient	46	16	10	20	52	56	58
Mansfield Town	46	16	7	23	50	65	55
Chester City	46	13	15	18	43	55	54
Swansea City	46	14	12	20	45	63	54
Wigan Athletic	46	13	14	19	48	64	53
Preston North End	**46**	**14**	**10**	**22**	**65**	**79**	**52**
Fulham	46	12	15	19	55	66	51
Cardiff City	46	12	14	20	51	70	50
Northampton Town	46	11	14	21	51	68	47
Blackpool	46	10	16	20	49	73	46
Walsall	46	9	14	23	40	72	41

1990-91 SEASON

THIRD DIVISION

Cambridge United	46	25	11	10	75	45	86
Southend United	46	26	7	13	77	51	85
Grimsby Town	46	24	11	11	66	44	83
Bolton Wanderers	46	24	11	11	64	50	83
Tranmere Rovers	46	23	9	14	64	46	78
Brentford	46	21	13	12	59	47	76
Bury	46	20	13	13	67	56	73
Bradford City	46	20	10	16	62	54	70
Bournemouth	46	19	13	14	58	58	70
Wigan Athletic	46	20	9	17	71	54	69
Huddersfield Town	46	18	13	15	57	51	67
Birmingham City	46	16	17	13	45	49	65
Leyton Orient	46	18	10	18	55	58	64
Stoke City	46	16	12	18	55	59	60
Reading	46	17	8	21	53	66	59
Exeter City	46	16	9	21	58	52	57
Preston North End	**46**	**15**	**11**	**20**	**54**	**67**	**56**
Shrewsbury Town	46	14	10	22	61	68	52
Chester City	46	14	9	23	46	58	51
Swansea City	46	13	9	24	49	72	48
Fulham	46	10	16	20	41	56	46
Crewe Alexandra	46	11	11	24	62	80	44
Rotherham United	46	10	12	24	50	87	42
Mansfield Town	46	8	14	24	42	63	38

1991-92 SEASON

THIRD DIVISION

	P	W	D	L	F	A	Pts
Brentford	46	25	7	14	81	55	82
Birmingham City	46	23	12	11	69	52	81
Huddersfield Town	46	22	12	12	59	38	78
Stoke City	46	21	14	11	69	49	77
Stockport County	46	22	10	14	75	51	76
Peterborough United	46	20	14	12	65	58	74
West Brom. Albion	46	19	14	13	64	49	71
Bournemouth	46	20	11	15	52	48	71
Fulham	46	19	13	14	57	53	70
Leyton Orient	46	18	11	17	62	52	65
Hartlepool United	46	18	11	17	57	57	65
Reading	46	16	13	17	59	62	61
Bolton Wanderers	46	14	17	15	57	56	59
Hull City	46	16	11	19	54	54	59
Wigan Athletic	46	15	14	17	58	64	59
Bradford City	46	13	19	14	62	61	58
Preston North End	**46**	**15**	**12**	**19**	**61**	**72**	**57**
Chester City	46	14	14	18	56	59	56
Swansea City	46	14	14	18	55	65	56
Exeter City	46	14	11	21	57	80	53
Bury	46	13	12	21	55	74	51
Shrewsbury Town	46	12	11	23	53	68	47
Torquay United	46	13	8	25	42	68	47
Darlington	46	10	7	29	56	90	37

1992-93 SEASON

SECOND DIVISION

	P	W	D	L	F	A	Pts
Stoke City	46	27	12	7	73	34	93
Bolton Wanderers	46	27	9	10	80	41	90
Port Vale	46	26	11	9	79	44	89
West Brom. Albion	46	25	10	11	88	54	85
Swansea City	46	20	13	13	65	47	73
Stockport County	46	19	15	12	81	57	72
Leyton Orient	46	21	9	16	69	53	72
Reading	46	18	15	13	66	51	69
Brighton & Hove Alb.	46	20	9	17	63	59	69
Bradford City	46	18	14	14	69	67	68
Rotherham United	46	17	14	15	60	60	65
Fulham	46	16	17	13	57	55	65
Burnley	46	15	16	15	57	59	61
Plymouth Argyle	46	16	12	18	59	64	60
Huddersfield Town	46	17	9	20	54	61	60
Hartlepool United	46	14	12	20	42	60	54
Bournemouth	46	12	17	17	45	52	53
Blackpool	46	12	15	19	63	75	51
Exeter City	46	11	17	18	54	69	50
Hull City	46	13	11	22	46	69	50
Preston North End	**46**	**13**	**8**	**25**	**65**	**94**	**47**
Mansfield Town	46	11	11	24	52	80	44
Wigan Athletic	46	10	11	25	53	72	41
Chester City	46	8	5	33	49	102	29

1993-94 SEASON

THIRD DIVISION

	P	W	D	L	F	A	Pts
Shrewsbury Town	42	22	13	7	63	39	79
Chester City	42	21	11	10	69	46	74
Crewe Alexandra	42	21	10	11	80	61	73
Wycombe Wanderers	42	19	13	10	67	53	70
Preston North End	**42**	**18**	**13**	**11**	**79**	**60**	**67**
Torquay United	42	17	16	9	64	56	67
Carlisle United	42	18	10	14	57	42	64
Chesterfield	42	16	14	12	55	48	62
Rochdale	42	16	12	14	63	51	60
Walsall	42	17	9	16	48	53	60
Scunthorpe United	42	15	14	13	64	56	59
Mansfield Town	42	15	10	17	53	62	55
Bury	42	14	11	17	55	56	53
Scarborough	42	15	8	19	55	61	53
Doncaster Rovers	42	14	10	18	44	57	52
Gillingham	42	12	15	15	44	51	51
Colchester United	42	13	10	19	56	71	49
Lincoln City	42	12	11	19	52	63	47
Wigan Athletic	42	11	12	19	51	70	45
Hereford United	42	12	6	24	60	79	42
Darlington	42	10	11	21	42	64	41
Northampton Town	42	9	11	22	44	66	38

1994-95 SEASON

THIRD DIVISION

	P	W	D	L	F	A	Pts
Carlisle United	42	27	10	5	67	31	91
Walsall	42	24	11	7	75	40	83
Chesterfield	42	23	12	7	62	37	81
Bury	42	23	11	8	73	36	80
Preston North End	**42**	**19**	**10**	**13**	**58**	**41**	**67**
Mansfield Town	42	18	11	13	84	59	65
Scunthorpe United	42	18	8	16	68	63	62
Fulham	42	16	14	12	60	54	62
Doncaster Rovers	42	17	10	15	58	43	61
Colchester United	42	16	10	16	56	64	58
Barnet	42	15	11	16	56	63	56
Lincoln City	42	15	11	16	53	54	56
Torquay United	42	14	13	15	54	57	55
Wigan Athletic	42	14	10	18	53	60	52
Rochdale	42	12	14	16	47	74	50
Hereford United	42	12	13	17	45	62	49
Northampton Town	42	10	14	18	45	67	44
Hartlepool United	42	11	10	21	43	69	43
Gillingham	42	10	11	21	46	64	41
Darlington	42	11	8	23	43	57	41
Scarborough	42	8	10	24	49	70	34
Exeter City	42	8	10	24	36	70	34

1995-96 SEASON

THIRD DIVISION

	P	W	D	L	F	A	Pts
Preston North End	**46**	**23**	**17**	**6**	**78**	**38**	**86**
Gillingham	46	22	17	7	49	20	83
Bury	46	22	13	11	66	48	79
Plymouth Argyle	46	22	12	12	68	49	78
Darlington	46	20	18	8	60	42	78
Hereford United	46	20	14	12	65	47	74
Colchester United	46	18	18	10	61	51	72
Chester City	46	18	16	12	72	53	70
Barnet	46	18	16	12	65	45	70
Wigan Athletic	46	20	10	16	62	56	70
Northampton Town	46	18	13	15	51	44	67
Scunthorpe United	46	15	15	16	67	61	60
Doncaster Rovers	46	16	11	19	49	60	59
Exeter City	46	13	18	15	46	53	57
Rochdale	46	14	13	19	57	61	55
Cambridge United	46	14	12	20	61	71	54
Fulham	46	12	17	17	57	63	53
Lincoln City	46	13	14	19	57	73	53
Mansfield Town	46	11	20	15	54	64	53
Hartlepool	46	12	13	21	47	67	49
Leyton Orient	46	12	11	23	44	63	47
Cardiff City	46	11	12	23	41	64	45
Scarborough	46	8	16	22	39	69	40
Torquay United	46	5	14	27	30	84	29